CAREER FULFILLMENT

ON THE ENLIGHTENED PATH

SCOTT E. CLARK

Bodhi Publishing Company, LLC
Phoenix, Arizona, USA

Copyright © 2016 by Scott E. Clark

Published and distributed by Bodhi Publishing Company, LLC

All rights reserved. No part of this book may be reproduced in any form or by any means, electronic or mechanical, including photocopying, recording, or by any information storage and retrieval system, or otherwise be copied for public or private use – other than for "fair use" as brief quotations embodied in articles and reviews - without prior written permission of the author and publisher.

The intent of the author is only to offer information of a general nature to help you in your quest for emotional and spiritual well-being. The author of this book does not dispense medical advice or prescribe the use of any technique as a form of treatment for physical, emotional, or medical problems. Each reader must address their own specific and unique physical, psychological, emotional, and spiritual needs and concerns, and whenever appropriate seek consultation with a licensed, qualified physician, therapist, or other competent professional for any advice, treatment, or diagnosis. In the event you use any of the information in this book for yourself, which is your constitutional right, the author and the publisher assume no responsibility for your actions.

Library of Congress Control Number: 2016920918
Tradepaper ISBN: 978-0-9903198-3-2
1st printing, December 2016
Printed in the United States of America

WITH GRATITUDE

I offer appreciation for all of the many teachers that have supported me within this human experience. Each has played a role in shaping my present reality and level of consciousness, leading to the message in this book series.

I also express my gratitude to all people who are endeavoring to live enlightened. The world needs your light in whatever unique form or method you have been gifted to provide it.

I forever acknowledge my greatest blessing in this life as the gift of my children, grandchildren, and family. You bring me so much joy, and make it possible for me to continue to heal, grow, and evolve, as I walk this journey of loving service and the sharing of Divine wisdom.

Thank you to Etana Holowinko (www.livesocietyjazz.com) for your talent and inspiration in the design of the cover, and for other technical and artistic contributions. Also, I would like to show appreciation to the great contemporary teachers of higher truth. And within the realm of business, I express gratitude to the many that are now creating and operating organizations based in greater consciousness and Unity.

TABLE OF CONTENTS

Introduction..1
Defining True Success..9
Higher Consciousness at Work......................................13

PART I: Inner Preparation for Outer Service...............17
Part I: Prologue..18
Part I: Energetic Quality or Tool....................................19
Chapter 1: Identifying with Your Authentic Self.............21
Chapter 2: Service is Your Deeper Calling.....................27
Chapter 3: Inner Assessment..33
Chapter 4: Discovering Purpose – an Inside Job............41
Chapter 5: Realizing Your Dreams.................................49
Chapter 6: Planning and Implementing Your Goals.........59
Chapter 7: Energetic Healing..71
Chapter 8: Developing Emotional Intelligence................79
Chapter 9: Claiming Higher Values................................85
Part I: Exercises...94
Part I: Affirmations...95

PART II: Promoting Wellness and Value at Work.........97
Part II: Prologue...98
Part II: Energetic Quality or Tool...................................99
Chapter 10: Job One: Getting Hired.............................101
Chapter 11: Job Two: Work Performance.....................107
Chapter 12: Enhancing Life Balance.............................111

Chapter 13: Time Management Considerations.............125
Chapter 14: Transcending Work Relationships.............141
Chapter 15: Cooperation and Unity.............153
Chapter 16: Impeccable Communication.............163
Chapter 17: Joy and Satisfaction.............173
Chapter 18: Surpassing Vulnerability.............179
Chapter 19: Healthy Approach to Compensation.............187
Part II: Exercises.............195
Part II: Affirmations.............196

PART III: Wisdom in Support of Career Fulfillment.....199
Part III: Prologue.............200
Part III: Energetic Quality or Tool.............201
Chapter 20: Career Wisdom – Discovery.............203
Chapter 21: Career Wisdom – Developmental.............209
Chapter 22: Career Wisdom – Realization.............215
Chapter 23: Leading with Integrity.............225
Chapter 24: Contribution Brings Greater Rewards.............233
Chapter 25: Applying Self-Awareness at Work.............239
Chapter 26: Career Growth and Ascension.............247
Chapter 27: Examples of Consciousness at Work.............251
Chapter 28: Career Classifications: an Enlightened View....257
Chapter 29: Supporting Unity in Business.............279
Part III: Exercises.............284
Part III: Affirmations.............285
About the Author.............287

INTRODUCTION

"Our finest moments are most likely to occur when we are feeling deeply uncomfortable, unhappy, or unfulfilled. For it is only in such moments, propelled by our discomfort, that we are likely to step out of our ruts and start searching for different ways or truer answers."

- M. Scott Peck

"On the Enlightened Path" is a metaphor for living your life within a higher perspective, through wisdom, mindfulness, and accountability. This is the title of this book series, and it applies to all aspects of your life. In this third book, *Career Fulfillment*, I am specifically addressing the deeper wisdom principles leading to satisfaction, meaning, and wellness within your work or career.

I am expressing concepts, in this book, that are in alignment with a deeper truth. Some of this information may feel like common sense, while certain terminology may seem strange or new to you. In any case, even while you may resonate with this empowering message, it is possible that you had not fully recognized this as pertinent to your career.

By including the topic of Career within this series on enlightenment, it is my hope that you will transcend some of the old outdated mindsets around work. And that you will be elevated and inspired to find greater fulfillment. As with any self-help material, it is always your responsibility to interpret this wisdom according to your unique path and consciousness. This is the beauty of self-help. I am simply a messenger.

Ultimately, the deepest truth that I am intending to convey is this: *You always have permission to operate and function within your highest energy and integrity at work.* However, YOU are the only one responsible for elevating your energy and perspective in order to create, live, and express your truth. Because of your personal interest in reading a book on this topic, I know that it is within your desire to create career success in this way.

My desire for guiding you with this wisdom comes from my assertion that there is quite possibly no human endeavor as fraught with the challenges of ego as "career." We all have experienced or witnessed countless examples of this truth, to the detriment of many. Within this aspect of life we deal with the issues of self-worth, identity, security, and competition with others for the material things we have valued (and consider limited).

Naturally, this message goes beyond the typical "how to get a job" and "how to make money." There are plenty of other books and authors that will focus on that. I will be taking a more expansive view of your career potential to include things like meaning and purpose, service and contribution, growth and abundance, wellness and achievement.

While there are some general characteristics and concepts that apply to all, the act of choosing a career, gaining employment, and earning a "sufficient" living is highly individualistic. Accordingly, your approach to career, and your definition of fulfillment (success) must be individually based as well. Therefore, an appropriate inner assessment must be a part of your process.

This may lead you to realize your most authentic and marketable skills. The fact is that some jobs and opportunities lend themselves to greater income and better working conditions than others. Accordingly, it is futile to compare our unique path with that of others, or expect that we all will create the same level of material wealth or position. Therefore, "fulfillment" is an expansion of the qualities and values that are desirable and more attainable to for you.

Regardless of your job or title – the quality of your work, the effort you put forth, and your ability to co-exist with other people – are all factors that bear great relevance to your success. And these are all attributes available to those who are focused on a higher, healthier view of themselves. A more enlightened perspective of your potential and purpose will help to you to align with the values that support you and all others holistically.

As you are able to shift your objectives and definition of success, your best path toward career fulfillment comes from elevating your consciousness at work. This is the result of inner healing and personal growth that affords a higher level of mindfulness and wellness. Thus, you are more supported in your expressions of the Divine energies: love, joy, peace, Unity, compassion, service, humility, etc.

These qualities of wellness are created within, regardless of your outer circumstances. Therefore, an ongoing focus on self-mastery must be developed and practiced. And this is the purpose of this book series that takes an enlightened view of your potential and purpose.

This material utilizes wisdom of a "spiritual" or holistic nature, within a practical application. It is intended to be inclusive of all beings, while promoting Unity and equality. In other words, I am neither endorsing nor condemning anyone's religious beliefs or practices. I am, however, promoting a message designed to guide and support you in living your human life with greater empowerment. Below is my favorite quote, which is highly applicable to my message.

"You are not a human being in search of a spiritual experience. You are a spiritual being immersed in a human experience."

- Pierre Teilhard de Chardin

As "spiritual beings," we have the opportunity to align with an identity, truth, path, and purpose that exceeds our typically limited ego perceptions. Or, what we have considered "reality." Accordingly, we may begin to intentionally allow for more loving energy to flow through us into all aspects of our human life – including career. Otherwise, while controlled by our ego-nature (to the exclusion of our truth), we will more often seek our own temporary gain at the expense of our higher fulfillment and that of others.

We have primarily been taught that we best meet our needs by striving and struggling, comparing against others, and winning our battles. This is some of the delusion that has created the worldly conditions from which we now must transcend. This causes us to reside within the lower energetic state of fear, which encourages great inner suffering.

My intention is to teach a message that helps you to awaken to a greater truth. Our evolution involves working to balance these two conflicting energies (love and fear) that exist within us. And our ascension will support us in offering and expressing greater value, integrity, service, and contribution to all.

Knowing that this holds the key to both our human survival and highest fulfillment, we may pursue a more enlightened reality. This becomes possible as you begin to notice with awareness when and how your energetic expressions are attached to either your Spirit or ego identity. One is based in love, and the other in fear; your thoughts, words, and actions will always define the difference.

Career Fulfillment

Since I am writing about "Career," let me tell you a bit about mine. I began my career by studying business in college. Aside from that general field of knowledge, I really didn't know specifically what I wanted to do for work. After my first year, I declared my major as Accounting, figuring that all companies need accountants and this would be a good avenue for gaining employment. I knew that I had an aptitude for this field of study, yet my decision was purely practical.

I never really thought about what was my passion, joy, or fulfillment. Even while "dabbling" in a few other jobs temporarily, I ended up working in accounting and management for thirty years. About half-way through I sat for and passed the Certified Public Accountants exam in Arizona. For about 16 of those years I worked within two different regional health insurance companies, as Controller and Vice President of Finance.

All told, I worked for several different companies in various industries, mostly small to medium sized. I also have operated my own bookkeeping business working with a small number of clients. Additionally, I have taught accounting and finance classes for small businesses at the community college level.

This was all a part of my professional path, which has both supported me and developed me for greater contribution. Over the past few years in the business, I knew that I needed to shift toward a career that fulfilled a deeper purpose and satisfaction for me.

In my experience, gaining employment is not an exact science. This is one reason why I am focused on offering wisdom that supports your overall life wellness, so that you can choose the path and career that resonates best with you. At times I was offered a job when I wasn't even looking for one; while at other times I searched for work for months while unemployed.

In any case, my life and career path has guided me to learn and experience many different work cultures. All of these experiences have aided me in discovering my truth, value, and purpose in the world. It also taught me the relationship between inner wellness and career fulfillment.

All in all, I realized a wealth of experience dealing with different conditions, circumstances, co-workers, management styles, industries, etc. Additionally, I have learned a great deal in the times that I have been self-employed or unemployed. My point is that there is no one perfect way to live your life or experience your career – it is always a process that will reveal your truth – if you are open to it.

However, the sooner you take an approach that honor's your unique gifts, qualities, passion, and interests, the sooner you will find yourself serving and contributing in the world with authenticity and integrity. The slowest and most unsatisfying path is to live someone else's dream, follow the crowd, or buy-in to the world's definitions of success.

As with all aspects of personal growth and evolution, you are accountable for all that you choose. Therefore, you must develop the self-love and inner strength to choose that which best honors your truth. You are here to share your incredible light AND achieve your highest fulfillment in doing so.

The first book from, **"On the Enlightened Path,"** was *Mastering Your Life*, which teaches the key concepts of Self-Mastery. And these three principles fully apply to your career fulfillment. First, of great importance is the identification with a higher truth – your Authentic Self – leading to the expansion of your perception of reality. Next is the development of mindfulness. Where, while connected to the present moment, you may make the most empowering choices for your well-being. And finally, as you heal, grow, and evolve you understand that you are fully accountable for all that you create. You now have a greater capacity to love and honor all others on their own unique journey of enlightenment. This is the basis for developing and supporting higher consciousness and Unity in your career and in business.

In addition to earning a living, I myself have learned many lessons about my own well-being, value, and personal evolution through my various work experiences and interactions. In utilizing the principles in the second book in this series, *Transcending Relationships*, you will have a greater understanding of the purpose and value of your relationships. At work, this offers the opportunity and necessity for many energetic exchanges with other people.

On a higher level, this is a great tool for healing, growth, and higher awareness. Depending upon your specific job, you may deal with co-workers, bosses, customers, vendors, or other related parties. How you are able to develop your emotional intelligence, and support the wellness in others is tremendously valuable to your success, and the quality of your experiences.

In the writing of *Career Fulfillment*, I have utilized many personal experiential lessons in wisdom, and have been guided to express principles of higher consciousness in the area of service/career. Consistent with the format of all of my books from this series, I am taking a 3-Part approach to support and guide you with information and inspiration as follows:

> **Part I) Inner Preparation for Outer Service** – Is a focus upon your inner truth and wellness as a means to claim your most fulfilling service and contribution. Through inner connection and assessment you will be guided toward an understanding and recognition of your authentic identity, deeper calling, and unique gifts, qualities, and purpose. Plus, I am offering further

wisdom about energetic healing, emotional intelligence, and higher values.

Part II) Promoting Wellness and Value at Work – Teaches you the tools for integrating and maintaining your higher qualities of energy within your work performance, interactions, and life balance. This includes time management, empowering work relationships, impeccable communication and cooperation. I also stress the importance of intentionally creating joy and satisfaction, and supporting growth by surpassing vulnerability.

Part III) Wisdom in Support of Career Fulfillment – Offers a powerful truth about your potential for elevating your contribution, rewards, and fulfillment. Learn to utilize higher consciousness by leading with integrity and applying greater self-awareness. I also offer wisdom on the value of growth and Unity throughout your various career stages and platforms.

Your highest capacity within this human experience is to live enlightened. When experiencing your career from this healthy awakened space, you may reflect the light of your truth into your service to the world. In this way you will ultimately achieve your deepest fulfillment and greatest satisfaction. You will literally shift the way in which you see yourself and the world around you. Your reality and consciousness will expand.

May this teaching guide and bless you within all aspects of your life, especially in the pursuit of career fulfillment and contribution.

DEFINING TRUE SUCCESS

"Every job from the heart is, ultimately, of equal value. The nurse injects the syringe, the writer slides the pen, the farmer plows the dirt. Monetary income is the perfect deceiver of a man's true worth."

- Chris Jami

How do YOU define success? How do you know when you are successful? Naturally, this term will mean different things to different people. Yet, is your success determined by you or by other people? Even if it is some combination of both, what should be your emphasis as you endeavor on the path of greater fulfillment and wellness?

Even when your external conditions remain relatively stable, one day you may feel like a success, and another day like a failure. So, what is it that influences our perceptions? Maybe, suddenly, a person, experience, or circumstance knocks us off our game. Or maybe we just feel differently due to the natural fluctuation in our energy or mental state.

In addition to defining the meaning of success, another question becomes, what is the source of your success, and how do you maximize this? Are you inner driven in the ways that are most supportive to your success? Or are you dependent upon others to confirm or judge you as successful? And, have you learned to include your personal wellness, satisfaction, and fulfillment into your definition of success?

For the most part, we have been taught that one's career success is determined by employment that contains one or more of the following: a high income, a prestigious title, power over others, or the admiration of the masses. If you are currently realizing any of these qualities, and are still reading this book, then maybe you have found this definition to be unsatisfying or unfulfilling on a deeper level. Otherwise, if you were perfectly satisfied with your career and life then you are probably uninterested in the message of this book.

However, if your career offers none of the above attributes, then you **know** that in order to feel successful you must expand this standard definition. You must learn to create and express the inner qualities of wellness and fulfillment as an intrinsic feature of your service to the world. Your career must support you in recognizing special qualities that exceed the opinions, approval, or rewards offered by other people. And the beauty of this approach is that, when functioning from this higher level, you are more inclined to offer real value to others as well.

I like to equate success with happiness. I have heard it said that, "happiness is the joy you feel when moving toward your potential." To me this describes an expanded view of career success as well. This involves creating inner wellness, which is aligned with your higher purpose and identity.

Otherwise, when you are overly motivated by external or material conditions, you are primarily striving for ego gratification – which is temporary and often dependent upon others. Whatever success looks like for anyone on the outside, it should bring inner satisfaction and fulfillment within, as well as, offer something of value to others.

My purpose in writing this book about Career Fulfillment is to express the message that – only you can define and create the conditions of success for you. The same is true for all people, as we are each authorized to live and

Career Fulfillment

create our best life. However, it is through identification with your Authentic Self that aligns you with the qualities and conditions that are most supportive to your well-being.

Each of the jobs performed by and for humans is meaningful toward supporting the needs of other humans. It is for you to decide which job is most authentic and fulfilling to your uniqueness. Some of these jobs will be more prestigious than others, and some will offer much greater monetary compensation.

This speaks to the value system in the ego world, and the economic conditions of supply and demand. Of course, this does not relate to your true value as a human being. If everyone could be a professional athlete, movie star, or corporate CEO, then even their conditions of worldly success would diminish. They would no longer be viewed as rare or special.

My greatest point is that for whatever we have to offer in service to the world, we are each to be valued beyond our salaries, titles, and acclaim. However, the system in place is very entrenched to either admire or admonish those of position and power. In either case, we are expressing the energy of fear. This is neither beneficial nor empowering. The best focus of our attention and intention is to heal, grow, and evolve within ourselves, and then become the positive force we wish to see in the world.

Therefore, I implore you to shift your focus toward defining and creating your own empowering view of success. Develop your work Presence, in alignment with your truth and mindfulness. Create a new work reality that is more beneficial to all involved.

This is the process and path of enlightenment! You recognize your career as successful by honoring your true authenticity and integrity. You create your greatest value and self-worth from your intentions, efforts, and expressions that offer sincere and compassionate service to others.

Certainly, there is joy in receiving the financial rewards and approval of others. This is especially true when it comes as a result of meaningful contribution. And, if this is available to you, it may be a part of your inner claim to success.

Most of us have observed within ourselves (and others) when we have given our service in a loving way for the sake of doing our best work. And we all know when we are selfishly giving minimal effort, while still feeling entitled to a paycheck (and even a pay raise). To me, any real definition of success requires integrity. And, in order to grow and ascend in our careers (and life), we must be able to be completely honest with ourselves.

I assert that while "getting paid" is a valuable and necessary part of working, your true satisfaction and fulfillment comes from doing your best and contributing something of value to others. I am no longer impressed simply by one's salary or title. What is most meaningful is the way people treat and support each other.

It is evident to me that an expanded view of success includes our ability to give and receive the higher qualities of love, joy, peace, abundance, and fulfillment. What has previously passed for career "success," is largely based upon the comparison of one's material affluence and power over others. True lasting success does not come from this ego-driven definition, but instead, in the development and expression of inner qualities that honor and support your best life.

HIGHER CONSCIOUSNESS AT WORK

"Remember, we all are affecting the world every moment, whether we mean to or not. Our actions and states of mind matter, because we are so deeply interconnected with one another. Working on our own consciousness is the most important thing that we are doing at this moment, and being love is the supreme creative act."

- Ram Dass

In the pursuit and performance of your career, you create fulfillment and best honor your true self by approaching it from your most conscious space. Consciousness is a terminology and state of being that represents your connection to your deeper truth. It is the perpetual "awakening" of your holistic senses.

This is the enlightened path that aids you in elevating your perceptions and intentions toward doing and being your best. You will function in higher awareness and loving energy. This is the place of your present moment power.

You are more authentic, and connected to your self-love and highest self-worth. Your expressions of energy (thoughts, feelings, words, and actions) are in alignment with your inner wellness and contentment. Now your spirituality is integrated with your humanity, and thus, you are more whole.

When you operate from this place, you are meeting your own needs with integrity. Therefore, you are less prone to being controlled by your selfish ego desires, or that of other people. Having accepted this potential as your reality, you now endeavor to re-align with this energy, or maintain an elevated state of consciousness as often as possible.

This may start, as was addressed in the previous chapter, with setting our work goals to encompass a more expanded definition of success. Because, if our goal is simply to "win" at all costs, we are functioning within a lower level of consciousness. We are less concerned about the consequences of our actions upon others, and ourselves long term.

Overly attached to the delusion of ego or human nature, we create a reality controlled by fear. In any given moment, an outcome in our favor seems critically important. Yet, if our intention is to be and do our best in a way that honors our integrity, we may create a deeper satisfaction in the effort and process of growth, development, and contribution; regardless of the outcome. You cannot do more than give your best, while not diminishing others.

Consciousness is a variable energetic state. We are never completely conscious or unconscious while having this human experience. The path of enlightenment involves a moment to moment awareness of your energetic state – or Presence. And then, as often as needed, you may realign to your Authentic or Higher Self. This is ongoing for those who are awakened to this truth.

Yet, when relatively unconscious, we are often unaware that we even have choices in how we express our energy. We will tend to revert to disempowering fear-based patterns, habits, and judgments. This is highly unsupportive to your wellness and that of others, at work or elsewhere.

Being conscious at work keeps you engaged, interested, passionate, empowered, and fulfilled. With awareness of your energy you will know when you have lost your connection to these higher qualities. Is it temporary, due to some natural fluctuation of your physical, mental, or emotional energy levels? Or is there something more that requires your attention?

Your effort to realign to your higher connection will be based on your inner assessment. You may need to create better balance, or heal some false and disempowering perspective or belief. Or, otherwise, you may be receiving a message that it is time to pursue some significant changes.

"I know of no more encouraging fact than the unquestionable ability of man to elevate his life by a conscious endeavor."

– Henry David Thoreau

We are always responsible for our own wellness, and accountable for our choices. Therefore, choose to honor your inner truth and take the steps necessary to restore and reinvigorate your best energy. You are meant to grow and evolve. This entails facing your vulnerability and leaving the comforts of the known from time to time. Higher consciousness supports the expression of your best energy – leading to greater growth and success along your path. And it is a necessary component for contributing and committing your best to others.

Any discussion about creating and experiencing career fulfillment must incorporate an awakening to a higher level of consciousness at work. This book is devoted to supporting you in doing just that. And when you elevate your individual consciousness, you are also elevating the collective consciousness in the world. Through the principle of Oneness we are all connected. This is a key truth on the path of enlightenment!

PART I:

INNER PREPARATION FOR OUTER SERVICE

"Your work is to discover your work and then with all your heart to give yourself to it."

- Buddha

PART I: Prologue

Within this enlightened process of creating and experiencing greater Career Fulfillment, Part I addresses the importance of a new focus and understanding of your inner preparation. This entails a teaching in wisdom intended to shift your awareness to accept that you have a higher identity, mission, and capability then you may have previously realized. You must be able to conceive of a greater reality before you can live it.

Your work is to be the outer expression of your best energy, gifts, attributes, and purpose. Therefore, you must go within to assess these qualities, and determine how they may support your choices. You likely will also be required to focus on a level of inner healing and growth, in order to shift your perceptions and create the opportunities and experiences that are most supportive.

From a higher perspective, career (or work) equates to **Service**. The work we choose, offers an opportunity to serve us and other people, on both a human and spiritual level. In pursuit of career fulfillment, this is your truth, your focus, and your intention. Regardless of your job title, the higher the quality of the energy you offer, the greater is your alignment with the principles that contribute to deeper success and reward.

Infused with an alignment to your greater truth, you are more motivated to pursue meaningful goals and dreams. You will develop the mindfulness to improve your emotional intelligence, as your efforts are also focused upon the success of others. As you are more connected to your own higher values, you will find greater fulfillment in both the process and result of your work.

PART I: Energetic Quality or Tool

The Energetic Quality or Tool most appropriate for inner preparation is *AWARENESS*. Yet, our awareness must be founded in truth and not delusion. Therefore, we will need an assist from **Wisdom**, which offers a higher message by teaching that you are authorized to be the master of your life.

This shifts your awareness toward the greater possibilities available to you, rather than the perception of fear, lack, and suffering, that may presently exist. It is very difficult to administer the power of awareness if we believe that we are basically unworthy or unaccountable for our lives. In truth, ONLY YOU are accountable, and your choices must reflect a willingness to honor this higher truth.

Your awareness may then be directed toward your inner wellness and the alignment with your unique gifts, qualities, and purpose. You will better understand your value in the honest assessment of your life; where you are, where you want to go, and how to get there. This leads to both, greater expressions of love for you and others, as well as, the creation of opportunities that are supportive to your success and fulfillment.

The opposite energy which often blocks awareness and wisdom is *IGNORANCE*. This is more than a lack of knowledge; it is the unwillingness to accept or consider things beyond your immediate experience or belief system. Through wisdom and awareness you may overcome ignorance, and awaken to expand your perceptions and level of consciousness. Take this opportunity to honor your process of inner preparation as you align your life to best offer your outer service to the world.

CHAPTER 1
Identifying with your Authentic Self

"You are very powerful, provided you know who you are."

- Yogi Bhajan

Your Higher Identity

Who do you think you are? There is a popular television show by this name, which presents various celebrities as they trace their family tree. I find it to be an interesting and entertaining show. However, I am not sure how it is relevant to how YOU live or define yourself today. The truth is that we are each on our own path of discovery, healing, growth, and fulfillment.

We are living our own unique human experience, and must learn to understand and honor our own truth. As infants, children, and young adults we naturally start out learning how to live other people's truths. Our education comes from our parents, family, and friends, our race, gender, and national history, and finally from the skewed values and agendas from the media. So really, who do YOU think you are?

If you too often find that you have a relatively disempowering view of yourself – you are not alone. As we are continually taught to judge and compare ourselves with others, one of two things happens. One, we feel inferior compared to those who APPEAR to have worldly success. Or two, we feel temporarily superior to those who APPEAR to have less worldly achievements. And in a relative way, we typically bounce between these two extremes.

Neither scenario truly defines your value, potential, and purpose in this life. You are not meant to be defined by others – whether you are condemned or idolized. However, this will often play into your false identity and become a barrier to your authentic truth.

How you perceive and express yourself in each present moment and each human endeavor will translate to the world who you think you are. And this creates your life experience and perception of reality. This is true for all aspects of your humanity, but within this book I will focus on the work/service area of your life.

In my experience and understanding, our self-perceptions go a very long way toward either limiting or expanding our opportunities and potential. When I take a higher view of myself I feel authorized to engage in the steps to manifest greater success and wellness in my life. Conversely, when I am down on myself and continually reinforce my inner fear, I am less inclined to pursue that which is most fulfilling and rewarding to me. I might even create or continue some form of experiential suffering through my fear and inertia. Can you recognize this as truth within your life?

We experience these self-judgements, for better or worse, as thoughts and feelings. Yet, in truth, they are forms of energy. All of our lives we have been energy receptacles. Our lack of higher awareness has allowed us to collect countless fearful, damaging energetic expressions from other people. Some so traumatic that we remain attached to this debilitating energy for many years. And we have turned this into our self-belief. Hence, regardless of our intelligence, wealth, or status, we are all in need of an awakening and re-training. And this must become our ongoing practice toward holistic wellness.

When connected to our wisdom we know that we have choices in how we express and maintain our energy in the present moment – based upon the awareness of our truth. This is how we begin to transcend our delusions and disempowering beliefs. We may now awaken to align with a true higher identity and unique life path.

As we shift our inner focus in this way, we become more capable of creating the fulfillment that we are seeking from our career. The question then becomes, are you willing to do this inner work? Are you willing to shift your perceptions of the "reality" you have been taught by other people? And will you elevate your energy in a way that honors both you and others?

As "spiritual beings having a human experience," our higher nature and identity is that which I call Spirit – or Authentic Self. I am not hung up on the terminology, and you may choose to refer to this by a different name. In any case, this is the part of us that exists on the level of energy, beyond our human senses. Therefore, we often have ignored or denied this identity as real, and we have become completely absorbed in the minutia of our physical existence and mental delusion.

Our Spirit exists before, during, and after our human experience (lifespan). Within this identity, we are an individuation of the Universal Life Force (some call God or Source), which exists only in the creative and expansive energy of love. The "made in the image of God" that we have heard of, refers to this energetic component, and is obviously not a physical resemblance.

Your Spirit knows your true path, potential, and purpose, unobstructed by the delusional limitations experienced within your human nature. Since this aspect of you functions on a higher/faster vibrational frequency, you must intentionally shift and elevate your inner awareness in order to align with your Authentic Self. Without any understanding or effort to do this, we continue to primarily reside in our lower ego-identity, which is based in the energy of fear.

Our spiritual and human existence is unique to each of us and runs concurrently, as we experience this lifetime – moment-by-moment. "Unique" should indicate to everyone that our paths will rightfully look different from each other. Accordingly, with a common energetic Source, yet a unique life path and purpose, we are all different but equal.

This truth authorizes us to both honor ourselves and ALL other humans; who are merely attempting to fulfill their own Divine journey and purpose. No one path is better or lessor than another, just different. Therefore, we are to recognize the Oneness of all life, which is an enlightened principle. And, until we do so, we remain stuck in our ego-nature that perceives great fear and lack, while expressing all manner of negative and harmful energy to each other.

Utilizing Your True Identity

Regarding all aspects of your human experience (including career), your higher nature and identity is a valuable place from which to begin to define your capabilities and potential. Therefore, I use these principles and terminology, not as mysticism or any kind of after-life considerations, but instead as a fundamental foundation for human success and fulfillment. You have this infinite part of yourself that knows your truth, potential, and purpose, which is based in the loving energy of all creation. Certainly this is more empowering than the definitions and self-judgment that you likely have learned in the ego world.

Therefore, is your best life enhanced by your identity defined according to your "problems, limitations, challenges, and inadequacies," as perceived in comparison to others? My answer is no. The truth is that we each are striving to overcome these things, and this is part of the human journey.

Career Fulfillment

Yet, how are we to transcend our challenges without awakening to a path that is not ruled by the very principles and beliefs that have enslaved us?

We all have an inferiority complex from time to time, and some people routinely live in this delusion. This is conditional, habitual, and fear-based, which is why an awakening to your higher identity and empowerment is often required. This must be followed by the ongoing re-training to your truth, and the releasing of the habitual thoughts and behaviors that create the conditions of fear and disempowerment. Some refer to this process as healing and growth.

You have been taught (directly or indirectly) that your human nature (and work agenda) is about survival of the fittest. We take from others before they take from us; we push them down the ladder and step on them in order to elevate our situation. This is all about ego and your false identity. There is a place for "fight or flight," as it relates to the protection of the human body. But we have taken this selfish philosophy and created competition that is both unsupportive of our true wellness and that of humanity.

As we evolve, we understand that ego primarily reinforces fear in its many forms. It is the lowest common denominator of humanity. It promotes anger, cruelty, and all manner of lack, greed, prejudice, and ignorance. As you become more fully awake, you will be amazed at how often it is used in business, politics, religion, and the media in order to control and disempower you.

So, maybe with a higher identification and education (in wisdom and enlightenment) we can do better individually and collectively. You can start by re-defining true success as alignment with your higher nature and unique life path. From this place you endeavor to create opportunities to serve in ways that are authentic and fulfilling on a deeper level.

You can develop a life plan that is designed to offer balance, wellness, and abundance according to your truth.

And you will offer your energy in a manner that is most loving and supportive of all others. This leads to service and contribution, which are requirements of career fulfillment.

Even after applying this wisdom training, you may not be surprised to learn that this is not easy. Change, growth, and ascension require effort and accountability. You have previously created an entire perception of yourself and the world (and called this "reality") based upon the delusion of ego. Accordingly, this energy is strong, and you will be pulled, through experiences and relationships, to return to this disempowering place often.

Some call these "tests," but really they are not judgements at all, they are opportunities. Through your awareness you will recognize these as examples of your false self that still exists, and your need for further healing and growth. Therefore, this is an ongoing transformation that is more than just an intellectual exercise. You are applying a new wisdom in order to redefine your reality. It is a consistent practice in mindfulness which will empower your awareness to support you in realigning with your higher truth.

As you become more successful in identifying with your Authentic Self, you not only begin to release your past false identification, but also your need to continually compare yourself to other people, or rely upon their approval. "Authentic" means true, "Self" means you – YOUR TRUTH. Therefore, within this identity you want to live according to your truth, not someone else's. When you focus your career pursuits upon obtaining the circumstances, conditions, and rewards that are authentic for you, you are honoring your truth and walking your best path. This leads to your greatest fulfillment and success.

CHAPTER 2
Service is Your Deeper Calling

*"The best way to find yourself is to
lose yourself in the service of others."*

- Mahatma Gandhi

What is Loving Service?

The best approach for creating meaning, fulfillment, and wellness from your career is to emphasize loving service. What does this mean? This involves your focus and intention upon offering service, as a natural expression of your loving, healthy energy. This is the service that is in alignment with your Authentic Self.

Having already discussed the significance of shifting to a greater view of yourself and your potential, this is the quality of energy from which you now endeavor to live. And functioning within your career (and life) from this perspective is the key to creating success and fulfillment. This is most supportive on a holistic level, meaning that you are growing and ascending on all levels of your Being.

So, why are you getting up and going to work every day? Is it in order to thrive within your new opportunity to perform your chosen job in a way that offers your unique gifts, talents, qualities, and passion into the world? If so, this is your higher service, regardless of your title, duties, or salary. With this is mind, you will find greater joy and meaning. You are more present and focused upon the quality of the energy that you express and offer to others. This is the loving energy that is highly conducive to success at work.

As you more often accept and function within your true identity, you will appreciate the greater significance of your work. Your elevated consciousness supports a more mindful approach and connection to the actual duties and interactions that encompass your work in each present moment. Then, through your accountability and integrity, you will create the best opportunity to enjoy the many internal and external rewards available. In this way, utilizing your career as your deeper calling, and a process of offering loving service, is a superior path to career fulfillment.

What if you ignore this opportunity to focus on loving service, and instead, expect that it is the responsibility of others to serve you? First of all, this does not represent your alignment with your Authentic Self or loving energetic wellness. Instead, this is attachment to ego, your lower energetic form based in fear. Additionally, this puts the quality of your well-being in the hands of others; a relatively disempowering state.

Higher Motivation

It is very important to become fully aware of your motivations for doing your work. Not only why you are doing this work, but also, what is the energy behind your choices and effort. And, is it effectively supporting your inner wellness.

As you more often intentionally connect to your inner truth you will more closely monitor your energetic alignment with your work. You will become aware of your true motivations. Do this not only to know that this continues to be the right work for you, but also to help you to maintain a higher level of service through the ups and downs of your daily job functions.

Career Fulfillment

Of course, historically we may have not taken such a holistic view of our jobs. We first and foremost have been concerned about our income and working conditions. In other words, we focused almost exclusively on the external qualities and rewards.

We are mostly interested in how we are impacted at work, rather than how we may impact others. Of course, I am not suggesting that anyone ignore conditions that are unsupportive or harmful. However, I am suggesting that when you are more whole within an alignment to your truth, you are both mindful of your conditions and focused on offering valuable service to others. This is your highest energetic state.

Therefore, what is it that you most want from your job? Do you value joy, meaning, and contribution, as much as material rewards? You know that you need your pay check to survive and fulfill your material needs. No one needs to talk you into that, it's a given. The real question is, beyond this, are you adequately considering the value of your inner rewards, wellness, and contribution?

Here's something to consider: of the following two scenarios, which is more likely. One, your motivation toward inner wellness, doing your job the best you can for its own sake, and offering loving service – leads to higher achievement, recognition, and abundance. Or two, your motivation for accumulating the largest salary you can in order to enhance your personal lifestyle – leads to personal fulfillment, love, joy, peace, and wellness.

I hope that you can see the opportunity to attain both inner and outer rewards by following a more enlightened path. This is always your path that is aligned with your higher identity, and connection to love. Yet, while attached and controlled by your ego identity, your path is limited and fraught with conflict and negativity. Additionally, your higher path is much more conducive toward encouraging and supporting wellness in others.

So, are you finding your fulfillment in the satisfying moment-to-moment process of performing your work at the highest level for the benefit of all? Or, is it in the potential to one day in the future achieve and receive some monetary goal? When your primary motivation leads you to honoring your highest identity and value, these need not be mutually exclusive.

A Focus on Service over Ego

What is typically unattainable is to experience great inner wellness and fulfillment while your entire focus is on what you can get, or what you need from others. How will you be able to experience and sustain inner satisfaction within a mindset that is overwhelmingly focused upon the rewards and benefits that are at the discretion of other people? I can tell you that you will be frequently frustrated toward others, and unfulfilled within. And, how unsatisfying is it to meagerly contribute real value, while still reaping financial rewards?

When we choose to view and function within our career from our ego-control, we can make work a very challenging place to find true success and fulfillment. As humans we have learned to embed our greatest fear in a lack of money/security. Therefore, we have created an inordinately fearful energetic focus around our work. And, this lower quality of our energy manifests into all of the negativity that we convey in the business world (greed, injustice, manipulation, discrimination, mistrust, etc.).

We have emphasized the obtaining of wealth and power over a desire to contribute something of true value to others. We promote self-importance, greed, inequality, and abuse. All of this stifles the energy of love and the true value of service – the qualities that are actually in alignment with our true identity. When we choose to hide our true power, we can easily feel lost and disempowered as we associate and lament within our fear-based delusion.

This does not make us evil or bad. But it has created a great collective unconsciousness and false training from which we are required to overcome. And this necessitates wisdom teaching, and our individual healing and awakening to a higher truth, potential, and purpose.

Placing your best energy upon the quality and deeper meaning of your service is intrinsically satisfying. You are offering your love and integrity which is expansive to you, and supportive to those with whom you work. Through healing and growth, develop and express the higher inner qualities of wellness in your life. And then, transcend your fear in order to express your loving energy at work as well. This is in alignment with your authentic truth and power.

As spiritual beings having a human experience, we must be accountable for attending to our needs on both levels. So for your greatest well-being, do not ignore either. However, you best serve both while in alignment with your Authentic Self. And you do not adequately serve your spirituality or support your humanity when controlled by your ego.

When you focus on the development of your self-awareness, self-love, and inner strength, you may be free to offer your best service for the sake of fulfilling your deeper calling. Your intentions are to honor yourself while contributing to the wellness of other people in some way. How this directly benefits others will be determined by them as they are able to receive your loving service. *Your focus is simply upon the giving.* Yet, for whatever that looks like, you are expressing positive energy and leading with integrity.

There is great inner satisfaction in offering your best service for its own sake. And this tends to lead to the highest quality of your work. Would it surprise you to learn that this is likely to be appreciated by your employer/boss, co-workers, customers, and other related parties? Does this not have great potential for leading to better pay and healthier work relationships? Additionally, when you complete your work for the day, you are better positioned to transfer your peace and satisfaction into your personal life experiences.

Releasing guilt or anxiety about your work performance (and the judgments from others) will help you to fulfill your other life activities more joyfully and effectively. Inner wellness and connection to truth leads to fulfillment and satisfaction within all aspects of your life. This is the purpose of self-mastery within the context of enlightenment.

You must be accountable for awakening and shifting your own inner perceptions and expressions of energy. You must heal, grow, and evolve, regardless of how others choose to function. Inner preparation for outer service is identifying and aligning with your own unique truth, value, and purpose. This entails transcending the energy of fear, and choosing to exist in the energy of love as often as possible.

The remainder of this book is dedicated to teaching and guiding you to shift and elevate your inner approach. Claim the wisdom that your Spirit knows as truth. This will lead you to greater Career Fulfillment.

CHAPTER 3
Inner Assessment

"I was always looking outside myself for strength and confidence, but it comes from within. It is there all the time."

- Anna Freud

The Value of Self-Assessment

Any intention to improve or elevate your life begins with an honest self-assessment. Self-mastery requires a high level of accountability. Otherwise, leaving your life to chance, or to the whims of other people, will ultimately prove unsatisfying. On the level of energy, you create the quality of your external experiences based upon your inner state. Therefore, your inner assessment is a crucial step toward gaining greater self-awareness, a precursor to healing, growth, and ascension.

Through insight we seek to realize our highest truth and purpose, and take an inventory of our present state of wellness (or lack thereof). Insight is defined as: "The act or result of perceiving the inner nature of things or of seeing intuitively." Rather than being considered "spiritual," which is too "woo-woo" for some people, the act of taking this approach is only logical and well-grounded to my awareness.

It is true that there are numerous tests and evaluations designed to assess potential career compatibility and possibility. And, while this may be beneficial at some point, the greatest evaluation involves "knowing thy self." And this is an inner journey.

You must determine your true gifts, strengths, aptitudes, interests, and passions. Since we are more often conditioned to avoid looking into ourselves in this in-depth way, be persistent within this endeavor. Otherwise, it's too easy to fall into a state of comfort and complacency with your dysfunctional habits and haphazard results. Or, maybe you are waiting for others to "fix" you or do your work. But that's not how enlightenment works. Your consistent accountability and participation are required when intentionally creating your best life.

Only you can know your true self, just as only you can shift to a higher realization of your potential for fulfillment. You must begin to determine if you are in alignment with the higher value that supports your best path. You came into this life to evolve and share your light in some unique fashion, therefore, do not abdicate your responsibility to align with this truth regarding your career.

Your inner assessment must be done in complete honesty – "To thine own self be true." This honesty involves your complete accountability and the stripping away of the ego-delusion that limits you according to your false self-judgments. You must adopt a view that recognizes your own light and potential, even in the view of your present circumstances and conditions. Evaluating yourself in this manner requires a connection to your Authentic Self.

Process of Inner Assessment

Create the space to allow for the highest view of your inherent qualities and potential to shine through. I recommend that you meditate and journal within this process of asking for guidance in your pursuit of insight. Aligning with your true identity elevates your understanding and empowerment. You are now most supported when you are willing to accept that you are always **enough**, and that life is always working through you (and not against you). For how supportive would be the conclusions of your inner assessment if you continue to perceive yourself through the cracked and stained lens of fear and doubt?

At times, within the development of our best career, we must be willing to consider two goals. One, what is my dream, calling, or purpose to be fulfilled in service to the world. And two, how am I going to earn my living. The ultimate goal is to create a career that honors and fulfills both things. However, this may be a process of many steps, beginning with your self-assessment – leading to personal growth and transformation.

So now, within your quiet meditative state, ask yourself pertinent questions, and allow the answers to come forth. Discover what resonates as truth for you. Here are some sample questions:

- What are the qualities that represent my greatest strengths and challenges?

- What are the activities and interactions that bring me the most joy?

- What services are I guided to share with other people?

- If I had no fear or perceived limitations, what would my work look like?

- What do I perceive as my greatest purpose to be fulfilled in this life?

- What do I perceive as my greatest obstacles to be overcome in this life?

- What are my true monetary needs – now and in the near future?

- How can I shift within in order to earn my living while fulfilling my purpose?

- What steps may I now begin to take as I pursue my best career?

Since we are all here to fulfill our own unique path and journey, the answers to these questions will be different for each of us. Work with your responses in order to gain more clarity. In the beginning, the fulfillment of our highest purpose may start with our understanding and promotion of our unique gifts and strengths. Then, as we recognize and overcome our own challenges, we may become aware of our opportunity to serve the world by supporting others who are facing similar difficulties. On a higher level, you may even come to understand that this was the very reason that you were so "aggrieved."

Enlightened living involves honoring your specific truth, and then designing your path around it. While the goal of success and fulfilment is universal, when we endeavor to find it without assessing our own truth, we will rarely experience the potential that is available to us. We may pursue the path of what we "should do" according to other people. Therefore, we will not realize optimal inner satisfaction and fulfillment **OR** offer our best service to the world.

Once you are empowered enough to recognize yourself without your distortion and attachment to fear, you may begin to determine your truth. In this moment, connected to your Authentic Self, you can observe the real you. You can hear or envision your Spirit's guidance. Are you beginning to become clearer about your best attributes

Career Fulfillment

and career path? If not, be patient and faithful, while continuing your efforts.

Compare this new insight about yourself to your present beliefs and career choices. And ask yourself the following questions:

- On the whole, do I enjoy my work and the benefit it brings other people?

- Am I offering my best integrity and intentions in the performance of my work?

- Do I earn enough money to sufficiently support myself and pay for the things I truly need?

- Am I satisfied with the quality of my work situation and my relationship to co-workers?

- Am I presently utilizing my gifts, qualities, and interests at work, while living a healthy, satisfying life balance?

The answers to these questions (and others) will confirm your connection to inner truth in relation to your current work. Regarding your answers in the affirmative, you are aligned with your truth, and may continue on this path with gratitude and fulfillment. You are intentionally and mindfully offering your career service while aligned with your higher energy – this is the ultimate path of success.

Yet, even so, as life shifts and evolves, you will need to continue to assess and monitor your energetic state relating to work in order to maintain this higher connection. And later, if you find that a change is appropriate, you will be aware of this truth before the external conditions become too negative or unbearable. You will have the power of choice and the inner-strength to honor your best insight.

However, if you find that your current job is not in alignment with your inner truth and wellness, you now have some work to do. No doubt, you already knew that there was a disconnection, due to the energy of fear, dissatisfaction, and a lack of desire, effort, or fulfillment. But now, having begun your inner assessment, you can work with your higher guidance and understanding of what YOU need in a job to be more fulfilled.

I hope that you noticed that I am addressing the significance of assessing your inner energetic qualities. You are best served by assessing your energy, which may be connected to either love or fear. This will bring feelings of relative empowerment or disempowerment. Self-mastery comes in determining your level of wellness independent of the perception from your outer circumstances.

Otherwise, what our lives look like from the outside may be heavily impacted by our ego delusion and the ongoing judgment of other people. For whatever the external experiences or circumstances involved, the real goal for you is to connect and align with your highest inner truth. Remain fixed within this level of mindfulness. This is what leads to the fulfillment of your unique purpose.

When you are unwilling or unable to assess your life, above and beyond your ego concerns and perceptions, you will be ineffective toward aligning with your deeper truth. With your focus on the external problems you will tend to blame other people, or become filled with self-doubt. And whether you remain disempowered in your current work or jump from job-to-job, you will not overcome your inner energetic challenges. Therefore, you must shift to a path of inner healing, growth, and ascension in order to claim your career success.

Further Analysis

As you proceed with your inner assessment, the goal is two-fold. First, now that you have a clearer picture of your best attributes, joy, and passion, you want to determine the job or line of work that honors this truth. In other words, what type of work may add to your bliss? What job or line of work might align with the flow of your highest energy, and most naturally aid you in offering your best service to others?

The second goal, as you continue this assessment, is in determining what is keeping you from receiving or performing this work that is potentially most rewarding for you. Your highest loving energy would always lead you to your greatest fulfillment (in all aspects of life). Therefore, what is the fear that is limiting your success? Where are you still connected to your lower identity, and how are you going to overcome it?

As you assess and begin to understand your specific strengths and challenges, you will become more consciously aligned with your inner truth. This supports you in taking the incremental steps to discover and otherwise qualify for your best work. Or, you may embark upon the energetic healing that has hindered your growth and wellness. This healing will be addressed more fully in Chapter 7.

In order to receive and perform most any job you must develop an appropriate skillset. This may involve an education and the practical application of your traits. In other words, there are specific actions that precipitate being hired and successfully performing any job.

Your inner assessment, first and foremost, assists you in understanding how your unique inherent qualities are best suited for certain types of work. It also gives you a clue as to where you need to further support energetic healing in order to more fully honor your truth. Your inner assessment is the best place to begin to create career fulfillment.

CHAPTER 4
Discovering Purpose - an Inside Job

"There is no passion to be found in playing it small – in settling for a life that is less than you are capable of living."

- Nelson Mandela

Your Purpose is Service

In truth, SERVICE is your purpose. This is true for all humans. Yet, as we have turned most everything upside down and made our egos our master, many people think more often of their desire to be served rather than their opportunity to serve others. When this attitude infiltrates your motivations and expressions at work it does not lead you toward fulfillment or value. And yet, fulfilling your true purpose is something that you came into this life to do.

Within the discovery and fulfillment of your purpose, your greatest prayer and mantra is simply, "How may I serve?"

Spiritual law dictates that what we give is returned to us, on the level of energy. So when you sincerely ask your Divine nature, how may I serve? The Universe's response is likewise, "how my I serve?" Your willingness to focus on integrity and the higher energy of loving service, will lead you to attracting that which you share, express, and offer others. This is, of course, empowering and supportive to your success and wellness.

However, it works the similarly in the opposite direction. Remember, there is no judgment within Divinity, only the consequence of the movement and quality of our energy. Therefore, when you intently and consistently focus your inner and outer expression on what you fear or lack, this energy is returned to you as experiences that bring more fear and lack.

This is not a punishment, and it is not anything that happens "to you." You are a creator within the parameters of your life. Therefore, you must be more accountable and mindful that the energy you express honors your higher state of being.

When you seek to serve from the space of love, you are connected to your Authentic Self, the part of you that knows your truth. From the standpoint of Spirit, this is a declaration of love, and supports alignment with your deeper purpose. This is the type of inner connection that will serve you best in determining, developing, and maintaining your best career path.

Regarding the above quote from Nelson Mandela, the choice to "play it small or settle" is about your willingness to grow, expand, and transcend beyond your self-limiting beliefs. Are you willing to shift your energetic expressions to their highest form? Are you willing to risk vulnerability in order to accomplish something of particular significance and meaning to you? Are you willing to discover and fulfill your purpose?

This is all about your inner evolution, and not about worldly rewards. Those with the greatest strength and love may be willing to sacrifice (or delay) wealth, comfort, and popularity in order to fulfill their deeper purpose and passion. The enlightened path is available to all, but not all will have the awareness and strength to do the inner work.

Service is a choice, just as it is a choice to express loving energy, and to heal, grow, and ascend in this lifetime. It is a choice to honor your higher self, and engage your true empowerment. Therefore, within the higher purpose of career fulfillment, the choice is not whether to focus on service, but instead, what is the service that best honors my truth.

YOU are Authorized to Discover your Purpose

Within your true higher identity and power you may create the ideal conditions for a meaningful and fulfilling life. Applying the principles of self-mastery supports you in discovering and living your true purpose. Regarding your career path this supports both the selection and performance of work that is most authentic for you.

Due to the fact that we exist in this world, we each have a unique purpose to fulfill. Accordingly, we are each authorized to discover this purpose, and create our best path of service. In order to identify and claim this higher calling, we go within to assess our inner energetic qualities and desires. This is the only direct path to finding your truth.

In addition to this tool, you may certainly network and engage in all sorts of connections with many other people. Over time, these interactions will offer you a glimpse of your truth, through contrast and agreement. However, since this is so inextricably mixed with their energy and your ego perceptions, it is a very indirect route to discovering your true purpose and path.

Unfortunately, we have been inclined to doubt our inner self, and instead, rely upon the opinions of others. Why is it so unnatural for us to trust our own knowing (truth)? It is because it so often goes against most of our worldly ego training.

In addition to denying our own intuition, we have readily accepted that other people are largely responsible for both our success and failure. So now, we are lost and utterly disempowered. Plus, we look at our past choices that led to suffering, and now may discount our own value.

Yet, in truth, your past choices were made under the delusion of ego, and not in alignment with truth. However, instead them being a critical mistake, they are sign posts designed to realign and awaken you. You are now to be more accountable to your loving truth, and choose to create experiences that support your wellness. This is all a part of your journey.

Again, judging your success (happiness, satisfaction, fulfillment, etc.) based upon other people or outside conditions is always a fool's errand. And like everyone else, I have made a life of creating and then overcoming this issue. I had to learn to be more accountable for my choices, experiences, and journey. And like me, only YOU can discover YOUR purpose and claim the greatest value in YOUR life.

The aspect of you that is connected to Divinity, and beyond the ego, knows why you are here and how you are to serve. When and how you acknowledge this wisdom is the only variable. Better to do this now, rather than to continue to grope through the outer darkness for the light switch within.

What is Purposeful Work?

To get the most out of life we must live it with meaning and purpose. The best way to do this is to create a career path that utilizes your highest gifts, skills, interests, and passion, within a balanced healthy lifestyle. Therefore, purposeful work is fulfilling to you on a level that touches your Spirit and humanity – your inner peace and way of life.

Career Fulfillment

Purposeful work is the demonstration of your contribution to the world.

Through the insight attained in self-reflection, you may have a clearer picture of what such work looks like for you. Or maybe you only have a piece of the puzzle at this time. Life is always a process of development. Typically, we are given what we need to begin, and the remainder is revealed through our continued insight, trust, and effort.

Likely, your self-assessment has identified qualities and interests that you would like to explore further. Continue to meditate on these, asking, **"How may I serve?"** Fill your subconscious with this mantra.

Briefly, just so that we are clear, purpose and meaning have nothing to do with lucrative, high profile, comfortable, or highly sought after. Service is service. And it relates to the offering of your authentic gifts, skills, and passion. Therefore, its value can only be judged by you and not by other people. If you choose to pick fruit, practice law, fix or sell cars, teach music, or anything else, do it in service to others and as fulfillment of your unique purpose.

Claiming Purposeful Work

Are there specific skills that you want to develop and share in service to the world? Can you envision a clear need to be served, and ways to either fulfill an existing position or create a new one? How does this work excite your passion? Do you feel a mix of peace, excitement, and vulnerability when you think about it? Because it is more meaningful to you, are you willing to transcend your inner fear, and put forth a greater effort to become accomplished? As you can see, only you can do this work!

There should be consideration of both your personal desire and the benefit to others. Does this work offer adequate or enjoyable working conditions for you? Does it appear that you could create a satisfying work/life balance in this career? Is this work readily available or do you need more specific training or education? Would this work require you to be an employee or are you more passionate about running your own business?

Since there are virtually an unlimited number of variables, it is critical to your success that you connect with the qualities that are most fulfilling and rewarding for you. Start by considering work that you most enjoy. Here are some of the options to contemplate:

- Do you prefer to work outside or inside?

- Would you prefer to primarily work with/on computers or equipment, or work directly with people?

- Do you want to manage people or simply be responsible for yourself?

- What hours or days do you prefer?

- What part of the country or world interests you most?

- Do you enjoy creative work, analytical work, sales or customer service, healing work, teaching or training, designing or building, working with animals, etc.?

- Would you prefer to travel, commute, or work from home?

These are only a few of the qualities and conditions of work to consider, and it is for you to determine what is most satisfying and personally rewarding.

Career Fulfillment

Consider if there is any line of work or specific job that you always secretly wanted to perform. Maybe you were discouraged by others, so you abandoned your dream. In this life you are here to fulfill your calling, and your inner truth knows this. Therefore, listen to YOUR truth, be courageous, trust the process, and be persistent.

As you begin to hone in on the line of work that seems to align with your purpose, you can start to consider various strategies for obtaining this work. You also can determine how all of this fits into your more human desires, like money, lifestyle, prestige, etc. Consider all of the factors that are most significant to you, but do this from your most sincere, empowered, and self-loving space.

This is wisdom that is connected to your Soul that must then be integrated into your human experience. Since we all function within different levels of consciousness, or connection to Spirit versus ego, this plays a role in our choices and will be unique for everyone. How you choose to balance your inner well-being with your ego desires is always up to you. Make your choices as best you can, but remain connected to your Spirit in order to assess the results of all that you choose.

Your compensation is largely based upon the external factors of supply and demand, opportunity, timing, etc. Yet, your inner focus on service and abundance consciousness will elevate your inherent beliefs and perceptions around money. And of course, your priorities and level of effort are factors as well. So, this is where your greatest input is relevant.

In my experience, a certain level of income is useful and necessary, but in and of itself does not correlate with satisfaction, fulfillment, or success. But this is a personal choice for sufficiency. Naturally, I will have a different determination of these levels than you.

How do YOU choose to balance things like compensation and status, with qualities like: freedom, stress or pressure, responsibility, enjoyable working conditions, healthy life balance, contribution to others, etc.? This is why it is critical to know yourself in order to make enlightened conscious choices. You are always choosing to balance seemingly opposing forces.

To get the most out of your choices, I suggest that you always choose to honor your higher truth in each present moment, and allow the future to manifest according to your best energetic wellness. Discovering your purpose is an inside job. Experience your life, listen to your truth, make choices based in love, and then continue to assess your energy. This is walking the enlightened path leading to Career Fulfillment.

CHAPTER 5
Realizing Your Dreams

*"The future belongs to those who believe
in the beauty of their dreams."*

- Eleanor Roosevelt

Self-Mastery is the Key

The key to self-mastery is to integrate your spirituality into your humanity. In the realization of your dreams you are essentially bringing into physical existence that which lives within your higher inner potential. This is more than an intellectual understanding; it also includes an experiential knowing and a process of creation.

This is not easy, nor is it simply a natural consequence of fulfilling your human needs. It involves significant intention, effort, and often a shift in your acceptance of what is possible. Yet, with re-training in wisdom, the application of mindfulness in the present moment, and absolute accountability for your choices, it is a worthwhile process on the enlightened path.

The reason that *Mastering Your Life* was the first book in this series is because it details the keys to enlightened living. And, whether or not you would ever think to use that terminology, it is a requirement in order to attain the highest fulfillment and success within any aspect of your human life.

This is really the meaning of integrating your spirituality into your humanity.

Within the context of this book, we happen to be talking about career fulfillment. Without utilizing wisdom, mindfulness, or accountability, your dreams are just fantasy, and your career is whatever job you can get to pay the bills. Therefore, an awakening is required in order to shift your energy, perceptions, and actions.

You must be willing to accept your higher identity, leading to the expansion of your awareness and connection to your truth. And this opens the door to the discovery of your purpose and realization of your dreams. Within your new understanding of work or career, you may now view this as your special and unique service to the world – your higher calling.

By the way, since we are each a part of the world, whenever you serve any of us in a loving way, you are serving the world. Now, through insight and self-awareness, you search within to assess and access your true gifts, qualities, interests, and passions that will support your dream career.

What are some of the inner-directed steps you may take in order to realize your dreams in this material world? You start with inner reflection, and then you may add the tools of affirmation and visualization, discussed below. Later, you will focus on the planning and implementation of your goals (Chapter 6). Though some of these may seem quite subtle, and your ego and impatience may question the value of such practices, you are developing habits and energetic shifts that will integrate and manifest your spiritual truth into your humanity. Any self-discipline exhibited toward these practices will pay dividends later.

In short, you are applying the tools, energetic qualities, and practices that are most supportive toward reaching your new powerful goals. Recognize that until you awaken and shift your energy into a direction that is supportive of your highest truth and wellness, you will only continue to create more of that which currently exists. Within this process, you are simultaneously endeavoring to realize your dreams, and working to eliminate the disempowering perceptions, energetic qualities, and activities that have previously hindered your fulfillment.

Meditation or Inner Reflection

Realizing your inner dreams is a part of your journey and purpose for experiencing your best human life. Therefore, become more accountable for implementing healthy, mindful practices that support both this higher purpose and your human fulfillment. As a way to shift your awareness into the present moment, I am a big advocate of meditation. In the *Mastering Your Life* book, I go into greater detail on this practice.

This is a training that you may undertake on a regular basis that is something positive and sacred that you can do for yourself. It is crucial that you begin to get comfortable being more present and connected to your inner space, beyond the distraction of your self-judgments, repetitive thoughts, and endless to-do lists. This simple, yet profound tool will support you in remembering to be more mindful throughout your day. Additionally, you may gain powerful insights and messages relating to your truth and unique path.

As you are learning to honor your whole Self, you must balance your time for "doing" and time for "being." A sitting or walking meditation is an intentional practice of allowing yourself to BE present with your inner truth. You are trying to create some space to connect with your dreams and higher path.

The point is to regularly create separation from the hectic energy of others, and from your normal unconscious habitual doing and thinking that is so often based in ego delusion. True mindfulness can be experienced in virtually any activity with practice; the key is to notice your thoughts and actions in present time. This, becoming the "noticer," is a form of recognizing the real you, apart from your ego. So endeavor to connect with your inner self as frequently as possible. You never escape your true self, and only avoid it at your own peril.

This meditation practice is a continuance of your inner assessment and the ongoing development of greater awareness. You have begun to grasp your dreams as your higher purpose, according to your inner knowing and truth. And now, the next step is to begin to recognize a greater association between your dreams and their potential for fulfillment. In order to realize your dreams you have to shift your inner beliefs, and conceive of a new reality in which they already exist.

Depending upon the specifics, you may require a significant shift away from how you previously have perceived your life, ability, and value. Having spent my career in accounting and management, this was the case for me in changing to writing, teaching, and self-employment. As one who has been relatively cautious in how I expressed myself (and slow to self-promotion), I was suddenly thrust into a job that centered on these functions.

Within the fulfillment of my dreams I have been guided to utilize my natural gifts and talents. Plus, it is essential that I continue to transcend my inner fear and commit to my growth and expansion. This is how we both honor ourselves and serve a higher purpose. I have been required to prepare and develop myself within before I was sufficiently comfortable in sharing my truth (outer service).

In order to live my unique path, I needed to more fully understand and accept the specific steps (inner and outer), as well as, allow for the most appropriate timing and unfolding of opportunity. I hope that you can see that this is not just a natural occurrence of maturity. This requires specific intention, great self-identity, practice, and patience.

Things that you will not find while following the herd or denying your special path and purpose. Your inner truth is more accurate for you than the opinions or examples of other people. And the timing of this healing and growing process will not necessarily conform to the desires of your ego. So, steadfastly do your own inner work and recognize your reward within the process.

For me, it has been a continual process of shifting and expanding, one step at a time. Though quite stubborn, my old identity and limiting beliefs are gradually transforming. Through my meditation and mindfulness I am able to confront my fears and barriers as they arise. Without this inner development I would never have been able to transition into my dream career (and life).

Having deciding that this is my calling and service to the world, it then becomes my challenge to determine how best to realize my dreams within the path that is in alignment with my unique gifts and qualities. In other words, I must create my own path. It is not enough to emulate other writers and spiritual teachers; I am not them, they are not me. And this remains an on-going part of my journey that requires awareness, openness, and patience. In truth it is always a bit of an experiment.

As a result of your inner assessment, maybe you don't require such a significant shift to realize your dreams. Yet, there is always work to do. Utilize your meditation process to aid you in the healing, growth, and development that is most supportive for you. Since "realizing" your dream is a moment-to-moment process, you always benefit from your deeper connection to your truth.

Affirmations

As a way to transcend your own fearful and limiting mental patterns, affirmations are a tool to shift your thoughts (energy) toward greater self-love and empowerment. There are two primary ways to use this technique. One, you may repeat a positive, loving phrase repeatedly in your mind as a way to bombard and saturate your subconscious mind with higher truth. You can make this a regular part of your healthy practice toward transforming your self-image and self-worth (i.e. re-training your mind). This would require a few focused minutes per day, especially when you first wake up in the morning and just before you go to sleep at night.

The second usage of affirmations would be as a replacement for present fearful thoughts as they arise. Your thoughts of self-judgment, doubt, lack, etc. are very disempowering, and serve to keep you stuck in mediocrity or worse. And after countless repetitions throughout your life, this has become your false identity. So, as you are now developing your awareness, and you notice a damaging thought, instantly affirm its positive opposite.

If you feel challenged in accepting the positive thought within your present "reality," then know that on the level of Spirit (energy) it is possible. You just need to fulfill the ongoing process of manifesting this new energy into the material world. Accept that you are now in the process of using this positive energy and creating a better human experience.

For example: "No one loves me" becomes "I am loved and lovable." Or, "No one will hire me" becomes "I am perfectly suited for the right job at the right time." Each of these positive statements is true, even if you feel that they are not currently present in human terms. You are worthy of love and of suitable employment, you simply are in process of creating a match. You are calling into existence that which you desire, as if it already exists.

Or, "I am a terrible _____ (artist, singer, or whatever your dream activity)" becomes "I am a Master _____, I am fulfilling my joy and purpose, and I am getting better every day." Even something like, "I am worthless (bad, hopeless, etc.)," becomes, "Every day in every way I am getting better and better." You must at least begin to conceive of the possibility of your healing, growth, and ascension in order to make it so.

All human experience begins in the form of energy. Therefore, you are shifting this energy to support the creation of your true desires. Honor your creative power to manifest your thoughts, words, feelings, and actions into the experiences that support your wellness and fulfillment.

If you go to work every day and say or think, "I hate my job (or boss, etc.)," you will only continue to attract the negative experiences that support your dissatisfaction and suffering. Therefore, be accountable for creating that which you DO want, instead of more of what you DON'T.

Also, be very conscious of how you use the term "I AM." This is a very powerful phrase that represents your Divine identity. "I am terrible at _____ (whatever it is)," is a personal identification with the negative statement, which helps to create and ensure that which it proclaims. This may be your habitual way of speaking, or even something you say in jest. Yet, my advice is to transform your habits and completely eliminate following "I AM" with any negative statement. Even if you are unable to go straight to "I am a Master at this," you can start with "I am improving and getting better every day." This begins to open your path to success.

Visualization

Within your meditation and affirmation work, start to visualize your dream as a present reality. As you begin to get clearer about the career service that is most exciting, authentic, and fulfilling to you, it starts to become more real. Build upon this realization by seeing yourself offering this career service that is your deeper calling.

In the law of attraction, visualization is a powerful part of the process of manifestation. Be as vivid and detailed as you can. Some people are more naturally gifted in this "seeing" than others, yet, simply do your best.

Try to feel that excitement and joy that you will experience when you fulfill this dream. It is this alignment with your inner joy and meaning that makes this a career worth giving your best qualities and effort. You can begin to value the experience of your ideal work within your inner awareness.

If you have chosen a career where you are less connected to service, and your primary motivation was to make a lot of money, you could not envision the same quality of enthusiasm for the job itself. At best your thoughts and feelings would center on the things that you could buy, or the prestige this may garner. This is rarely enough to sustain you in creating and offering your best energy and contribution, and therefore, is not aligned with your higher values, integrity, and purpose.

The truth is that overcoming our self-made obstacles are always a part of the process of fulfillment, and your inner and outer efforts to see yourself as successful are always valuable. Yet, even within this visualization and affirmation work, you need to hold a space for accepting what comes. The best mantra for this becomes, "this or something better." You are putting forth the higher energy to manifest your dreams, which is spiritual work, so now you must allow for things to show up as either fulfillment or further guidance.

Today we are attempting to create from our best awareness and consciousness. As we move forward on our path of ascension we may find the cause to adjust our desires and goals. So maintain a mentality that is more open than

Career Fulfillment

fixed. Be firm on your focus of self-love and higher potential, but allow for the specific path and details to manifest as they will. In the realization of your dreams, utilize your loving Presence to work within your current circumstances as they arise, while keeping your intention upon service and alignment.

CHAPTER 6
Planning and Implementing Your Goals

"Nothing can stop the man with the right mental attitude from achieving his goals; nothing on earth can help the man with the wrong mental attitude."

- Thomas Jefferson

The Holistic Approach

Planning and implementing your career goals is part inspiration and part perspiration, as it has been said. We make a plan that aligns with our truth and supports us in achieving the next step on the path of fulfillment. And then, through our efforts, we perform or otherwise complete the tasks designed in our plan. This fulfills the key principles of Self-Mastery – wisdom, mindfulness, and accountability.

Implementing your dream job may be a very involved process of inner transformation and outer growth that requires many steps. In other words, some dreams will take great effort and faith to achieve. Therefore, you will want to identify various incremental steps along the way. Within your primary focus, plan the next step in the process, while still holding some vision for the grand achievement. The well-known parable applies: How do you eat an elephant? Answer: One bite at a time.

For other career dreams you may be endeavoring to make the next logical progression from the job you currently perform. Or, your goal is to simply perform your current job with more skill and joy. In any case, you begin by shifting and healing within, and then you develop your plan for implementing the steps to accomplish this dream objective.

You are focused on defining both the inner and outer steps necessary to shift your energy toward creating the opportunity you desire. Within this phase you are more present, and intentionally choosing to love and honor your true self – consistent with your inner motivations for realizing this dream. Whether or not you have previously considered or attempted this ascension, your inner assessment and development is now elevating your self-belief, and you begin to move in the direction of fulfillment.

This is the process of "creation," although you may not have thought of it in that way before. Yet, what you are working toward will manifest according to a timeline that may be unknown to you in this moment. Therefore, in addition to choosing love, you must trust the process; especially when the realization of your dream requires the involvement of others in some significant way. This often entails great patience, perseverance, and focus upon the things that you can control.

Additionally, as you expand your energy in the direction of growth, you will encounter your self-created monster called vulnerability. In order to continually defeat this inner delusion of fear you must apply courage and considerable amounts of self-love and self-trust. This is where many people give up their dreams.

If while present and loving you have the energy and awareness to create a powerful thought or take a specific action that directly leads to the achievement of your goal, you will do so. Otherwise, each loving energetic expression is a link in the chain of implementing your dream. This leads to each new step in this process of manifestation in the material world.

You may not know the extent of the path or number of steps involved. So your mission is to be present, loving, and simply do your best. And this is why your inner motivation, aligned with your higher nature, is so very critical.

When we revert to our fear-based expressions, we temporarily break a link in this chain. Therefore, endeavor through mindfulness to realign to your truth and replace this negativity with loving energy as quickly as possible. Use your meditation, affirmation, and visualization tools.

Without a sufficient connection to your Authentic Self, and the true higher purpose in attaining your dream career, it is likely that you will succumb to fear, doubt, and impatience. You may prematurely abandon your dream when some other new shiny distraction presents itself. It is as if we are looking for reasons to undermine our own truth, instead of re-enforcing it.

While your energy is primarily attached to your ego-nature and lower identity, you will find comfort in settling for something that offers less than your true inner satisfaction and fulfillment. We can justify or blame all we want, but the truth is that we chose to abandon our dream and higher purpose.

You may think that all of this "spiritual stuff" is too much work, and that you are just going to continue on your current path. This is not uncommon, and certainly a choice available to you. But common lives do not create true fulfillment or the achievement of your highest purpose. Your life path involves healing, growth, evolution, and higher service, regardless of a denial of such things.

You are presented with experiences within your humanity, created from your energetic expressions, which are opportunities to choose to love and honor your higher truth. These "callings" will continue to come, encouraging you to awaken to your power and responsibility for creating your best life. Implementing your dreams is most fulfilling because it requires the best you have to offer yourself. Settling for less than your best is always unsatisfying because within your truth you recognize a level of failure.

Collegiate Goals

If you are starting your college "career," your ultimate goal is obtaining your degree of choice. Although, I realize that if you just recently finished High School, your goals probably also include experiencing freedom and the pursuit of fun. However, the achievement of your degree is a relatively long journey with many steps (tests, classes, semesters, etc.), and you cannot always anticipate all of the variables in life. So, within a more mindful process, know your ultimate goal, but focus your energy on implementing your plan in present tense.

Attend your classes, study the material presented, gain guidance and tutoring where needed, pass your tests, and complete the course. Learn to find achievement in each step fulfilled, and in the higher value received in the process – knowledge, experience, and accomplishment. In this way, you are naturally and successfully progressing toward your overall goal of graduation. Being mindful and appreciative within the journey will add to your life the greatest sense of fulfillment and success.

Does this make each day or step easy and joyful – no. There are often obstacles to your peace and happiness that you must transcend. Sometimes it is directly within your control to take an action and improve your situation. And at other times you must accept "what is," make the best of it, do what you can to improve your effort or attitude, or even just weather the storm. This is always a temporary affliction, so, within your loving presence you can more quickly re-align with your truth and empowerment.

Career Transitions

The higher wisdom principles of planning and implementing your goals are certainly true regarding significant career changes. I previously mentioned my goal of transitioning from a long-standing career in accounting and management into writing and teaching. I had dreamed about writing for many years, and I always found great satisfaction and fulfillment in discussing personal growth and spirituality with others as the occasion presented itself. But this career change really only existed as an idea or mental fantasy, until I decided that its realization was possible.

This was not only a new career path, but quite clearly a major redirection of my own self-identification. This involved great inner preparation for outer service. I have been required to implement my dream through all of the fear and vulnerability that has arisen within. My process is ongoing, but my best focus has led me to honor my truth within this career endeavor.

Let me highlight some of my process for the planning and implementation of my goals. Even if your goals are different, this may give you some guidance or wisdom in support of your process. Wanting or thinking about writing books and actually doing it are two very different things. So, I needed to utilize my whole being in this endeavor; my spirituality and humanity, my heart and mind, my intuition and intelligence. It required a shifting of my identity and self-belief, the right timing, personal space, financial support, discipline, courage, and more.

Millions of people have written books, even self-help inspirational books. However, it is not within my higher alignment to try to copy or impersonate another author/teacher. While I knew the type of books and authors that were most rewarding and enjoyable for me to read, I had to discover and create my own path if this was ever going to be fulfilling and successful for me.

I knew that my truth came from my life experience and spiritual training, and this would somehow form my message and content. And I trusted that if this was my purpose, and I pursued this work with my best energy and integrity, then at some point the audience, students, and clients would manifest. After all, my true purpose is to serve, therefore, if I am guided in this way, there must be people who would benefit from my contribution.

I already had exhibited a certain sufficient level of writing ability. So with this as my starting point, instead of sitting through endless classes and workshops, I decided to just jump in and start writing. I was willing to learn from the actual process of writing. In truth, much of your personal fulfillment and success will more readily occur as you display the courage to simply begin. Yet, all of these considerations were part of my inner assessment.

I determined that my goal was not to learn from others how to write my book, but instead to express the truth that resonates and flows through me. I trusted that this ongoing effort would naturally lead to my initial goal of writing my books. At times I wrote significant portions of books, only to discontinue them and start over later. While listening to my inner knowing, either the material or the timing was not right for me. But I continued to trust the process.

Then, about a year after I published my first book, I was inspired to create this book series. I started with a list of the various topics or aspects of the human experience that are most significant to each of us (career, relationships, health, etc.). Areas of life fraught with dissatisfaction and suffering that would shift to a healthier, happier experience as a result of a more enlightened approach

This would be my purpose and motivation for writing this book series. And then, one book at a time, I wrote an outline which I felt covered the central ideas and message within the topic. From there I wrote (and then re-wrote many times) the specific content as it came into my awareness to write.

I researched how to publish a book, and followed the steps involved. And I worked with outside contractors for the few things that I could not do myself. So, my overall dream is to write and teach this material that has been so inspiring and supportive in my life. But my plan primarily involved completing each step in the process leading to this overall goal.

For me, writing has been an easier, more natural way of communicating than speaking, especially to larger groups or audiences. Therefore, my plan directed me to start there. I personally know people who are more comfortable with the speaking, who later hope to write their book. So the main point is to create your own path, which honors your unique gifts and talents.

My plan included writing the book series, one book at a time, and then afterwards I would shift my focus toward the teaching and promotion part of the business. I have found that the world primarily tells you to promote yourself first and last, and to gear your products/services around obtaining the greatest sales volume. But this felt inauthentic for me.

Nothing wrong with getting paid, we all need money. Yet, fulfilling your calling is about more than that. There is a strong element of healing and growth that must precede true career fulfillment. This is an enlightened PATH, not a sudden thrust of your personality into the limelight. And yet, in truth, there is a balance of steadily climbing hills and stepping off of cliffs, which you will need to manage for yourself. Take the experts advice (marketing or otherwise) with a grain of salt, and learn to follow your own intuition.

Regarding my own career fulfillment I am practicing what I preach. I am teaching that integrity and authenticity within your primary motivation are most conducive to your personal success. My goal is to offer my service in ways that are most fulfilling to me, and this has brought peace, joy, and meaning to the process.

Always design your plan in a way that is most supportive for you. If you are unsure about this, your inner assessment and reflection will guide you. Even if this is contradictory to the advice of others, work in ways that are in alignment with your truth. At the end of the day, only you are responsible and capable of realizing your dreams.

As for the writing, I began to write the words that "came through me," one paragraph, page, and chapter at a time. Nothing happens without the writing, so this was the daily implementation of my plan. Within the current book I was working on, I either chose to write or not to write each day. Even with the goal of publishing books, my focus and service is about writing.

I enjoyed the accomplishment of writing, both for the inner reward and fulfillment and for the production and progress it demonstrated. I was implementing my plan. Due to the nature of this work, it is often isolated from direct feedback and recognition from other people. Therefore, I was required to utilize my inner strength, self-love, and personal accountability in order to sustain me.

In truth, outside encouragement was shockingly sparse. Yet, there were a few individuals who were instrumental in boosting my resolve to keep writing. Ultimately it was up to me to appreciate my own efforts and achievements, which is a valuable lesson for all. This is YOUR dream, and not "theirs."

As I am presently writing this – my third book in the series – I remain focused upon the plan of writing and publishing, and then will work more directly with other people as a way to support and guide them toward their growth, wellness, and success. Within my plan, this is the next phase of my higher service in the world.

Of course, there are no guarantees of how any of this will work out in the end. That is how life works. Yet, I am finding such joy and fulfillment in this process that I have no regrets regardless of the final outcome. I love the actual work, and not just the attainment of any external rewards. And that is how enlightened living works.

Whatever is your plan, it needs to be most supportive of your goals (short and long-term) and aptitudes. There is always a combination of learning how other people have done the things that you are attempting to do, and simply jumping in and creating your own process. There is no easy or safe way to accomplish something great and meaningful to you. I have structured Part I of this book as I have because the best advice I can offer is to make sure that you are pursuing your dreams, and not someone else's.

You are authorized by your Divinity to access your higher knowing and purpose – so start there first. Discover your purpose and then implement your dream through an inner connection to your best loving energy and power. Develop your plan according to your own unique gifts and needs.

You will find aspects of your journey that are very natural and authentic for you – again, start there. And there are many things that you will need to incorporate into your skillset along with way. Your plan involves inner healing, maintenance, and growth in order to progress through your fear and vulnerability. And it also involves connecting and associating with other people whose support you will need.

Implementing your career, like life itself, is always a moving target. You make choices and express your energy in each present moment the best you can, based upon your awareness and understanding at the time. So you are wise to emphasize the visualization and planning for that which is most readily attainable. When you are walking your enlightened path, you use wisdom, mindfulness, and accountability to support your healing, growth, and wellness day-to-day.

From this space of awareness and evolution, you may create and revise (or refocus) your plans as is most appropriate and supportive for you. This again, is the ongoing integration of your spirituality with your humanity. How do you know when to shift and change your plan versus when to hold true and persevere? Unfortunately, this is not as black and white as we would like. However, your inner energetic wellness will give you the inspiration and clues you need. Your job then will be to trust this wisdom as guidance.

Evaluate your outer relationships, interactions, road blocks, and unexpected disturbances from an inner-energetic perspective. While each of these circumstances is likely to bring a dose of fear, sit with this feeling for a moment. Now, release your attachment to a particular outcome or expectation and find a more objective space from which to ask the following questions: "What is the truth of this situation?" "What is this teaching me?" And, "How am I to proceed in a loving manner?"

Your inner truth will support you with the answers you need in order to go forward consciously and most empowered. Learn to recognize your inner voice, apart from your perception of the energy of other people. Endeavor to offer the greatest self-love and acceptance for your journey. You are discovering and fulfilling your true purpose.

You may be guided to press forward or make minor changes to your plans. An adjustment may be necessary due to your awareness of some temporary inner vulnerability that has been upset by someone or something. Weather this situation with your best presence. Re-connect to your truth and power, and commit to staying the course.

Career Fulfillment

If, however, within your inner assessment you recognize a desire to make significant changes to your career plans, you want to verify from where this guidance is coming. Are you simply abandoning your dream because your fear got the best of you? Or are you shifting your timeline in a way that is more supportive toward implementing your dream? Or, through an inner awakening resulting from a higher understanding of this process and your truth, are you beginning to identify a new dream?

When you are awake, you learn, heal, and grow through the process of living your truth. Once you learn what you need, you are sometimes directed onto a new path. All of this works for your higher good, even if you don't recognize this at the time.

Use awareness and planning to keep you connected to the truth of your path. You are invested in the quality of your experiences when you understand your accountability for creating them. Stay as focused and connected to mindfulness as possible, and honor the process leading to the highest outcome available to you.

Think big with respect to your potential and the unlimited nature of possibilities that exist. Do not limit your dream to the results of past perceptions and experiences. However, since your power is in the present moment, be keenly aware of today's potential for inspiration and production. Whether you are someone who likes to write out detailed action plans or simply visualize your plans, honor your best gifts and unique qualities.

There is no one plan or one way to plan that fits all. This is why the focus of my message is to guide you toward connecting within. This is not only the place to start, but also the place of healing when you experience set-backs or discouragement. Your path is for you, even though it is designed to support other people in some way. So take the initiative to discover, visualize, and plan your dream service.

CHAPTER 7
Healing Your Energy

"It is better to conquer yourself than to win a thousand battles. Then the victory is yours. It cannot be taken from you."

- Buddha

Focusing on your Energy

Whether you are focused on career fulfillment, transcending relationships, or holistic wellness, your highest achievement is always dependent upon the quality of your energy in any given present moment. We are never once-and-for-all "healed," instead, we are forever "in process" of healing, growth, and transformation or evolution. In this life, we are always functioning within various energetic states, that in one form or another, are either expressing love (connection to Spirit) or fear (connection to ego). And the results of these expressions either support our higher truth, or reveal the need for further healing.

With respect to envisioning, creating, and honoring higher service in your most purposeful career, your awareness of energy is vital. It signals your intention for living enlightened, and offers the best opportunity to reclaim your power and correct your course as needed. You will not only live more fully within your own power, but you will be less inclined to attach to or create negative encounters with others. Within the practice of mindfulness you are living each moment in the awareness of inner wellness or your need for healing and expansion. This is a reflection of higher consciousness, personal accountability, and empowerment.

Maintaining Healthy Energy

First and foremost, we all are in need of inner healing. This does not diminish our value. It is actually part of our purpose in having this human experience, as it is leads to our growth, evolution, and service. Even as one who espouses the benefits of living more enlightened and conscious, I still consistently create and attract experiences that highlight my need for energetic healing. This is true for all humans.

From these experiences I may notice my thoughts and feelings being moved to a level of negativity and disharmony that disrupts my inner love, peace, and wellness. When this happens I must look not only at the energy directed toward me from others, but most importantly, what is it within me that allowed this attachment to their expressions in a negative way.

Within this wisdom you may grow to accept the expressions from others as relatively neutral, regarding its impact upon you. It is the power that we ourselves assign to their words and actions that then shift our own energy for better or worse. And this echoes our present connection to self-love or fear.

Do we engage with other people who are at times insensitive, lacking awareness of others, critical or demeaning to us? Yes. This is how energy is expressed when someone is connected to ego (fear). And since this is an issue for all people, do not be so surprised when it is directed toward you. It is primarily reflective of them and not you.

This does not make anyone evil. It simply reflects their need for inner healing in that moment. From a more enlightened perspective we can understand and accept this, for this is something that personally afflicts us from time to time as well.

As you become aware of this "invasion" to your energetic contentment, your first step is to gain the realization that this expression is primarily an issue within the person challenging you. And their temporary delusion and disconnect need not determine your wellness or identity. Even while there may be ongoing consequences in certain situations, it is your focus on inner calmness and empowerment that will be most supportive to you. And ultimately, it may be a supportive reflection of energy for them.

Therefore, your intention and effort toward refraining from personalizing this expression is exceedingly valuable. As Don Miguel Ruiz says in his wonderful book, *The Four Agreements*, "Don't take anything personally" (this is the second agreement). I highly recommend this book for all who are seeking a more enlightened path.

The Process of Healing

Yet, for the times when you DO attach your energy to their negativity (and you will), the process must turn inward toward your healing. This does not always supersede the requirement to deal with an impending consequence, but it is a key to your transformation and wellness. In this case, at least on a subconscious level, you have chosen to connect your energetic state to the negative expression of another.

This will have the impact of depleting you energetically. And may likely diminish your self-esteem, causing your ego nature to flare up and defend itself. Even if your reaction is loud and fiery, it leaves you in a weakened capacity. You have shifted into defense/attack mode, which is based in ego (fear), and you have temporarily detached from your Spirit (love).

In this instance, the words (spoken or unspoken) or actions (and even the inaction) of another has resonated with some false and disempowering self-belief. A part of you is fighting to refute this on the outside, yet within, you secretly harbor this negativity. This is what you need to recognize with your mindfulness. And this is the part that needs your healing intention.

All of your past experiences and interactions with others have impacted your perception of yourself, including your identity and view of your potential. The repetition of this deception effectively hinders you in certain present-day experiences. And, for those with a higher sensitivity to the energy of others, this is even more debilitating. This necessitates the need for healing now.

Energetic healing is the transformation and elevation of energy that is stuck in some false and disempowering belief.

Your job is to clear this inner belief that is trapped in your energy body (mental, emotional, or physical). When we choose not to pursue our healing in this way, we simply continue to experience the suffering, stagnation, or disappointment that our diminished capacity creates. Yet, with awareness, you may utilize your present experiences and encounters to show you your journey to healing.

Understanding that we each have a unique human path, our level of wellness or need for healing varies. All that makes up your human experience is a part of your Spirit's plan for healing, growth, and ascension. Within my statements, I am not diagnosing, prescribing, or counseling. I am offering a pathway of wisdom and accountability that may lead you to greater transcendence and fulfillment.

Career Fulfillment

From a more holistic perspective, our energy bodies exist on the physical, mental, emotional, and spiritual planes. There are those who may assist your healing within any of these areas. However, in truth, it is your own wisdom, mindfulness, and personal accountability that will have the greatest impact to your healing process. Others will have little or no real impact in support of us if we ourselves are unconcerned about our responsibility for our wellness.

Be vigilant as to when and how you are damaging or supporting your own energetic wellness. We are miraculously designed Beings. Listen and pay attention to your body, your thoughts, and your feelings. These offer expressions of energy that relate to your state of inner wellness.

With awareness, you will recognize when you are either functioning within a supportive energetic flow, or otherwise, sensing some disturbance that needs your attention. You may not have associated this as energy before, yet, develop your awareness to notice these things as such. Even though your energy is impacted by others, it belongs to you exclusively.

For those who presently feel the burden of great inner suffering, it is likely that you have ignored your energetic warnings for an extended period time. And consequently, the negativity tends to mount and infect all areas of your human experience. You may have been unaware of your own power to create or facilitate your own wellness. Or, through delusion, you have identified with the many false and disempowering teachings that have devalued you.

Wisdom is the antidote for both ignorance and delusion, which is why it is the first of the three key principles to enlightenment. And wisdom is a necessary part of energetic healing as well. Only you are authorized and empowered to support your own wellness. As only you are able to monitor and assess your inner energy, and then, as you notice that you are attached to fear, you may realign with your higher truth.

Much of our ego training has caused us to do two things that are unsupportive to our energetic wellness. First – we ignore the warning signs and trudge through the pain, exhaustion, depression, delusion, etc. This may be especially true for men, who historically have judged it as weakness to "look inward" or develop the sensitivity needed for awareness. In truth, choosing to disregard wisdom is the very definition of ignorance.

Secondly – when we do admit that there is some disturbance that may be in need of healing, we are more accustomed toward blaming the problem on outside sources or conditions. In doing this, we are absolving ourselves of accountability – but also are denying our own power to heal and elevate our life. Then, in a relatively disempowered state, we are resigned to hoping and waiting for outside circumstances to change, which is a false premise. Instead, it is always your responsibility to recognize your truth about creating and resolving your energetic issues.

People go from job to job, and relationship to relationship, always viewing the other person or circumstance as the problem. But their need for inner healing goes wherever they go. Only you can create the conditions for healing your energy, and thereby, improve your external circumstances.

Example of Healing a Work Energy Disturbance

Throughout this book I will discuss various specific issues and examples of addressing your energetic healing, and how it is the optimal solution for your external problems. However, I will give you one example here:

While dealing with work, notice when you are experiencing the various energies of fear (including: anger, powerlessness, selfishness, greed, embarrassment, doubt, complacency, etc.). You are likely associating this disempowerment with some outside person, circumstance, or experience. Yet, it is the energy of fear that resides within you that is the source of your problem.

This fear is expressed as expectation and judgment, but it reveals a lack of self-love or value. Again, this does not mean that there aren't very unconscious and delusional people out there. It simply means that you have the power to heal yourself and negate their influence upon you.

Learn to shift your focus toward what you need for healing, growth, and ascension. Hating your boss or co-worker for some perceived injustice is not resolving the situation or healing your energy. And will eventually cause problems in other areas of your life as well.

The fear is simply a sign of some inner disturbance that needs your attention. Find the answer to the "real problem" within and then be accountable for taking the appropriate steps to resolve the conflict without.

Depending upon what you need in order to facilitate your own healing, you may decide to evaluate your past experiences, thoughts, and feelings. You must be cognizant of releasing any present identification with your past suffering, or otherwise, you may connect to a false victim identity. You are not reliving the experience, you assessing it for clues about the genesis of your inner fear today.

Recognizing your past, with a new higher mindset leads you to learning and transcendence. This is the application of wisdom. You are intending to dispel the myth that you are in some way deficient, unworthy, or unlovable. Sometimes we can do this on our own, and at other times coaching or counseling is most beneficial.

Start by bringing your full presence into this present moment, use your breath to become more grounded. Focus on defining your capabilities and potential in the light of your current level of consciousness and greater self-love. Remember, within your higher identity, you are a spiritual being simply having a human experience. It's rarely, if ever, life or death.

So, take this perspective that affirms that you are more than your perceived problems, challenges, or failures. You are simply creating an experience as a consequence of your need for inner healing. Utilize this higher awareness to realign to greater self-love and self-trust.

Within your inner preparation for outer service, your inner state of wellness is critically important. As part of your assessment toward connecting to your truth, notice the fear and self-doubt that pops up. While not getting stuck in this energy, know that you will eventually need to address and heal this at some point.

This may become necessary as the result of an experience that occurs in which you will be required to deal with your fear head-on in present time. Or you may be able to heal it proactively, before any "crisis" occurs. Just know that in order to reach your greatest success you will not be able to avoid this.

Healing is a normal process of your development and growth, and it is your "problems" or difficulties, arising from your energetic expressions, that alert you to your need to heal and shift your energy. Be self-aware and courageous in your willingness to be accountable for your own healing. Utilize coaches and other healing practitioners that may assist you in your process. Learn to be the greatest advocate for your own wellness, and endeavor to consciously live within your best energetic flow.

CHAPTER 8
Developing Emotional Intelligence

"There is zero correlation between IQ and emotional empathy...They're controlled by different parts of the brain."

- Daniel Goleman

What is Emotional Intelligence?

A key advantage in working on "inner preparation" is that this supports the development of greater *Emotional Intelligence*. This is a term used in the science of psychology, and is defined as follows – "The capacity to be aware of, control, and express one's emotions, and to handle interpersonal relationships judiciously and empathetically."

This isn't just a "try harder" or "be smarter" thing; the work that you do in healing your energy and elevating your consciousness is the greatest determinant for this development. Your focus and growth in this area will greatly support both personal and professional success and fulfillment.

Emotional intelligence (EQ) is commonly defined by four attributes[1]:

1. **Self-awareness** – You recognize your own emotions and how they affect your thoughts and

---

[1] Definitions from HelpGuide.org

behaviors. You know your strengths and weaknesses, and have self-confidence.

2. **Self-management** – You're able to control impulsive feelings and behaviors, manage your emotions in healthy ways, take initiative, follow through on commitments, and adapt to changing circumstances.

3. **Social awareness** – You can understand the emotions, needs, and concerns of other people, pick up on emotional clues, feel comfortable socially, and recognize the power dynamics in a group or organization.

4. **Relationship management** – You know how to develop and maintain good relationships, communicate clearly, inspire and influence others, work well in a team, and manage conflict.

Can you see how this is wholly supported when living within a more loving-enlightened connection to life? Conversely, when disconnected from your higher truth, and ravaged by ego, how could you possibly function within a high level of EQ?

Does this not sound like monitoring and healing your energy within, and more consciously expressing your energy out to others in each present moment? Even with slightly different terminology, the previous chapters have been guiding you to heal and grow in ways that elevate your emotional intelligence. And, no matter what career you choose, this development is crucial to your fulfillment.

Emotional intelligence is something that we can improve upon, since it is essentially a learned skillset. It helps us turn intention into action, in order to make informed decisions about the things that matter most to us, and to connect to others in productive and nurturing ways. The enlightened path is all about doing just that. It is applying wisdom, mindfulness, and personal accountability for the sake of creating and living your most authentic and empowered self. And this is the energy that supports Unity.

Applying Higher Awareness in Support of EQ

Self-awareness is a key to building emotional intelligence. Remember, emotions (feelings) are a form of your energy. And to be aware of your moment-to-moment connection with your changing emotional experience is the key to understanding how emotion influences your thoughts and behaviors. Your various expressions of energy work together to reveal your inner state of wellness in light of all experiences that show up.

At times this emotional expression will instigate stress. So how do you best deal with this? It always starts with your awareness in the moment. You feel what you feel based on some external experience that triggered an inner disturbance. Of course, this represents some fear or negativity that you are holding within. Typically, this comes from a past experience that left a harmful impression, which is now coming forth to impact you in the present. It is in this moment that you are not only aware of your emotion, but also your need for healing.

Depending upon the situation, this could be a lot to handle all at once. If you feel overwhelmed in the moment, it is your level of emotional intelligence that will either support or diminish your wellness. When in control, you may be encouraged to gain some distance from the situation and resist the inclination of responding with energy that reflects your inner wounds.

Be sure to focus on your breathe. Find the mental insight to shift to love, peace, and compassion for yourself and anyone else involved, as quickly and thoroughly as possible. Then, in a more suitable environment, take the time to reflect on the truth of the situation.

Look for a solution that supports your inner healing – this is the recognition of spiritual truth. You have previously chosen to attach your identity (and emotions) to some false energy (information, accusation, judgment, perception, etc.). And now with a more enlightened view of your loving truth, you have an opportunity to release this fear-based delusion.

You no longer need to "defend" yourself to others. In truth, you were merely defending your right to give away your power, and continue to create this form of emotional suffering within. And, from the space of your Authentic Self, you certainly would not desire to bring suffering to another.

With your greatest focus upon your holistic wellness, regardless of what anyone else has said or done, your best intention is to express the energy of love (peace, truth, wellness, understanding, and healing) to all involved. The energy expressed to you from all others reflects their beliefs and perceptions, and need not define you at all. Therefore, when your focus is upon your own healing and elevated emotional intelligence, you will more easily accept other people as they are without allowing them to negatively impact your experience and wellness.

Applying Mindfulness in Support of EQ

Always seek to maintain your mindfulness, which is the practice of purposely focusing your attention on the present moment. This brings a sense of calm, as it transforms your typically unruly and uncontrollable thoughts into a greater appreciation and experience of "what is." You become more self-aware of your truth and more open to the truth of others. And this supports a higher perspective on life.

Social awareness is keenly connected to mindfulness. In order to be supportive and attentive to others we must be present. Otherwise, while stuck in our heads – planning, analyzing, judging, etc. – we are virtually unaware of our surroundings and connections with other people. And, we are primarily focused on getting our own selfish needs and desires met.

We are not presently noticing our expressions of energy, which while unconscious, may reside in the negativity of ego (fear). Nor are we picking up on the subtle non-verbal clues of others. Proper social awareness demonstrates a level of appreciation or caring that may be felt positively by those in whom we intend to connect.

"People don't always remember what you do or say, but they will always remember how you made them feel."

– Maya Angelou

You are actually more likely to further your personal and professional objectives by setting aside your thoughts, intentions, and goals, and focusing on the interaction itself. Present moment awareness is an empowering personal process. You are able to "take the temperature of the room." In other words, recognize your surroundings and audience in order to be most effective with your words and actions.

Your interactions are to be a give-and-take process that utilizes your best attention, intention, and consideration. Some may think that in paying attention to others they are diminishing themselves. But the opposite is true. Paying attention to what you experience emotionally, as you listen to others, may illuminate your beliefs and values – for you.

Through your connections and interactions you may learn something important and valuable about yourself. Within every relationship there is an exchange of energy, and you must be open to receiving what these others have to share for your benefit. It is no coincidence that they are in your life.

As you continue to accept and expand your deeper truth, you enhance your own self-confidence and self-worth. This aids in your ability to open your heart and awareness to all of life around you. You may truly acknowledge that, like you, all people are on their own unique path of healing, growth, and ascension.

Therefore, as you become healthier and more loving within, you will be more accountable for your own choices and well-being. Accordingly, you will offer greater attention, caring, and compassion in support of the well-being of others. This is an example of integrating your spirituality into your humanity in the development of emotional intelligence.

CHAPTER 9
Claiming Higher Values

"Happiness does not come from a job. It comes from knowing what you truly value, and behaving in a way that is consistent with those beliefs."

- Mike Rowe

Career Fulfillment and Values

Your values ultimately become your destiny, and are the results of your thoughts, words, behavior, and habits. Therefore, higher values are more than just some arbitrary and biased moral code, invented by past generations. It relates to the quality of your energy and the creation of a more loving and empowering reality.

This is consistent with the idea of elevating your definition of success, as was discussed in the beginning of this book. In your pursuit of this higher definition, be certain to claim (live) the values that promote this deeper meaning and integrity.

Value is defined as something intrinsically important or desirable. The meaning of intrinsic is, "Belonging to the essential nature of a thing – occurring as a natural part of something." Therefore, it is the job you choose and the way you serve in this job that aligns with your higher truth and values, which intrinsically leads to career fulfillment.

So, how are YOUR current values aligned with your higher truth, leading to career fulfillment? Do you need to elevate your values and offer more love and integrity in your current job? Or, is it your job that is not in alignment with your highest purpose and wellness?

True fulfillment will support you in the enjoyment and wellness of your life, on all levels. It does not come from playing games or manipulating "the system" or other people. Nor is it based upon the approval from others, whether family, friends, the media, or the public at large. Instead, it comes from living your own authentic and unique path with enjoyment, purpose, and higher intentions for all.

Within the construct and maintenance of a fulfilling career, living your higher values requires that you apply and offer both your spirituality and your humanity – on a daily basis. This is quite a commitment. And this is why your career is to represent your deeper calling and support your evolution within this human experience. From the population of all potential jobs, you must determine and perform service which provides and offers the greatest value to you and all others.

Values versus Morals

To be clear, while values and morals have been recognized as synonymous, I have been guided to comprehend the distinction. Where I see *values* as the quality of our energetic expressions, I understand that *morals* represent the way in which this impacts us and others. Clearly, these two do intertwine often.

You cannot simultaneously treat another person or group unethically (immorally) and claim to live higher values. So, values are not simply something you espouse, they are representations of how you express (live) your life. Healthy values support a more positive treatment of us and each other, while distorted and delusional values are mostly harmful to all life. The difference is that in our world, "morals" seem to be judged by others according to beliefs, which vary greatly.

Values, on the other hand, are more intrinsically defined and experienced. Are you presently endeavoring to promote love in all that you express? You are then living higher values and your morality will follow suit. Yet, if you are promoting fear (hate, judgment, discrimination, etc.), you are living lower values and your morality will be low as well; regardless of the "high-grounded" authority you may claim.

From the perspective of Spirit, higher values honor the energy of love and all life. For example, "Love thy neighbor as thyself," or "Do unto others as you would have them do unto you," are values not beliefs, regardless of who said it. All other judgments of supposed morality are either extraneous or serving human ego.

Assessing and Elevating your Values

It is imperative that you fully understand where you have chosen to place your value (quality of energy) in relation to career. When you primarily (or exclusively) value the things that prop up your ego, such as wealth, status, appearance, popularity, and extravagant lifestyle, you will create experiences that are more in alignment with this pursuit.

You may think, GREAT, that's what I really want from my career. And of itself, this represents lower values. Even if you are able to achieve these goals, you may be missing the deeper meaning and opportunities that higher value delivers. While not emphasizing the value of offering your loving service and contribution to others, you are not aligning with the energy that brings joy, peace, and fulfillment from your work.

In any case, you may claim to be "successful," and recognized as such in the world. And, you can even claim to be in alignment with your values. However, these lower values are based in fear and not in unconditional love. Therefore, the benefit to you and others is limited by energetic law. Of course, this truth is clearly apparent, as we witness the behavior and results in the world today.

This is not a judgment against material prosperity. Not all people of means and power have achieved their status through selfishness, greed, or ruthlessness. And, many wealthy people of achievement have committed to great service and support of others. However, these loftier pursuits are reflective of their higher values.

In confirming that this is not a "rich and poor" thing, certainly, just as many people of lessor means struggle with their fear-based beliefs. This is rooted in lower values as well. As we each are able to elevate our values and pursue a more authentic and loving approach to career, we will live and create lives aligned with greater peace, joy, prosperity, and fulfillment.

When I talk about claiming lower values that emphasize a willingness to use and abuse others for selfish gain, I'm not just talking about fat-cats on Wall Street, CEO's, or politicians. Certainly, they represent many examples of this behavior since the beginning of time. However, it is the more subtle examples that afflict regular people, like you and I, which need to transform.

Maybe our goal is to just "get ahead" and gain some advantage or reward in a way that lacks integrity. After all, this is the way of the world, right? No argument there. However, on the enlightened path you are transcending the habitual expression of energy that is both harmful to others and less than the values inherent in your true Authentic Self.

This, of course, is a process of development (healing, growth, and ascension). Yet, within your wisdom, awareness, and accountability you must sincerely endeavor to elevate to higher values in all that you do. It is your higher value that brings the fulfillment of your higher purpose and evolution.

We all must be willing and able to recognize within our own lives where we are falling victim to lower values in pursuit of ego gain. This will take great honesty and personal integrity. On one level (or many) this has caused us to judge and mistreat others – and devalue ourselves. This is not only clearly harmful to humanity, but it is disempowering to us. It literally blocks the energy necessary for us to create the rewards that we truly desire.

Accordingly, even if we win a few battles and receive something desired from work, it will not have the impact we expected toward enhancing our true inner wellness. And we will soon find ourselves back into the space of dissatisfaction and in pursuit of the next thing that we believe will bring us happiness. When functioning in lower values we never seem to receive enough; not enough of the material rewards we desire OR the inner peace, joy, and fulfillment.

Again, within the offering of lower values we are mostly focused upon what we may receive from others in order to satisfy our material desires, rather than what we can contribute. The highest energy in existence is love, which expands as it is shared. Therefore, as we naturally pursue deeper inner wellness as our ultimate reward, this is not possible without the values that contain love.

All Souls are here to ascend to the higher possibilities of their human experience, in whatever form their uniqueness provides. Lowering your values equates to limiting your expressions of energy and therefore the quality of your reality. It makes the concept of deeper meaning through service nearly unfathomable.

With an absence of love, peace, compassion, Unity, generosity, service, and holistic wellness in your value system, you will maintain an overabundance of fear, greed, dissatisfaction, entitlement, judgment, ignorance, discrimination, stress, and lack. To me, a lavish lifestyle and well-stocked Balance Sheet are insufficient compensation for a life of fear.

Seek to develop and nurture the values of love, and aspire for inner prosperity first. Judge not your "value" based upon your material life. As you claim your higher values you will express the energy that is more effective toward achieving your best quality of life. From here, you will have greater appreciation for all that you earn. Endeavor to realize YOUR potential and not simply be envious or critical of those with a different path.

As we elevate our values we each must awaken to the deeper meaning and purpose of our career – ask yourself the following questions:

- Independent of my income and material possessions, what is it that is most meaningful and purposeful to me?

- Regarding the people in my professional and personal life: how am I serving them with love (instead of fear and judgment)?

- How can I separate my unique "needs" from my "desires" in order to expand my opportunities for happiness?

- How might I define career fulfillment that is more attainable and meaningful to me?

- What values and conditions are more supportive to my overall holistic wellness?

- What are the values that support a greater level of love and consideration for ALL other people?

- How may I express the energy of these higher values within my career and life as a whole?

Career Fulfillment

Living in the energy of your lower values creates a life stuck in fear – the true culprit of both immorality and the devaluation of human life. Within this lower level of consciousness, the values you express at work (energetically) are likely more self-centered and self-protective. Or maybe, you will decide that since you cannot achieve your ego-based desires you will avoid work altogether; thus, requiring others to provide for you. Ego says, "If I can't get what I want, I will take yours (directly or indirectly)." This is an example of lower values leading to a reality that is unsupportive to all.

When you are not contributing your best energy in both fulfilling your material needs and in offering your service to the world, you need to shift and elevate your values. This can only be done on an individual basis – within yourself. This is one of those times that you must set aside your judgment about the lack of higher values in others, or the unfairness and inequality in the world.

Be fully accountable for you! You cannot instantly change the whole system or other people; you can only choose to either elevate or lower your energy and perspective about life.

While "the enlightened path" is not about terminology, I like the word *abundance.* This relates to a whole spectrum of qualities and attributes supporting spiritual and human wellness. And this may introduce the concept of "ENOUGH," as it relates to the material resources that meet your human needs. Career fulfillment (a quality of abundance) comes from serving a useful and valuable purpose, and offering your best gifts, passion, and energy to others. Additionally, abundance relates to holistic health, peace, and happiness, which comes from integrating your Divinity into your humanity through higher values.

Once you understand the difference between your material needs and desires, you can work toward creating your reality within the healthy balance that represents "enough." Your focus is now upon redirecting and aligning your values to support your true definition of career success. Your needs may be more minimal than previously thought, and your desires can be managed within an overall consistent expression of your higher values.

As you are contemplating all of this, you can evaluate your current work, or otherwise investigate new work that is in alignment with your deeper truth. Your pursuits are now connected to your expanded values. As opposed to primarily desiring higher incomes at all cost, you now prioritize that which adds to your greater happiness and contribution. You now consider the overall condition of your inner wellness (peace, health, joy, abundance, meaningful service, etc.). Is your career enhancing or diminishing these things?

Typically what I have noticed when work simply becomes a money grab is that most people shift into the mindset of doing the least amount of work possible in order to sustain their income. Or, they make a big "show" and exaggerate the value of their work in order to elevate their status. Within these mindsets work becomes intrinsically unsatisfying. It is now a chore that offers very little value or fulfillment.

This is a disempowering attitude that negatively affects us, regardless of salary level. And it is unsupportive and uninspiring to co-workers. We have either limited or lowered our values, and are very likely experiencing dissatisfaction at work (and at home). Does anyone see this as successful?

When claiming higher values, the very nature of the work, and quality of your participation, can offer the potentials of joy, peace, self-worth, and achievement. Your best job may offer the conditions of love, acceptance, well-being, life balance, and an environment in which you may thrive. And the compensation can be such that you deem it a fair exchange for your services, while it affords you sufficient living conditions.

Career Fulfillment

What if your work is enjoyable and rewarding to your inner being, yet you can't earn enough money to support your basic human necessities? Then, this cannot be your best job, at least at this time. As we define and list what is ultimately most valuable to us, we cannot ignore the necessity to at least provide for our basic material needs.

This does not mean that you choose to do something that dishonors yourself or is in direct conflict with your higher values. So, even while you pursue greater income, you can lead with integrity and positive energy. This is an example of being fully accountable for your success and wellness. However, you need to continue to be mindful of your ultimate pursuits, and not simply forfeit your dreams because you got comfortable and content with money over fulfillment.

In order to claim your highest values, determine what is most meaningful and rewarding for you. As you approach your career in alignment with your truth, you develop the conditions of your success. Your ongoing work is to trust yourself through the challenges, and stay the course. We are all here together, functioning within this world – so awaken to your enlightened path.

My success is not dependent upon your suffering or failure. And in fact, within the collective consciousness, my life is actually enhanced by your fulfillment and ascension. This works well when the greatest priority of my values is in alignment with the inner qualities of love and wellness. Therefore, through love, elevate your values and transcend the delusion of fear; encourage and support career fulfillment for all.

PART I: Exercises

1) Within your sincere space of higher connection and solitude, utilize the process of inner assessment as you seek guidance in support of your truth. Are you able to gain more clarity about your unique gifts, qualities, interests, and passions that may fundamentally support your higher service and career fulfillment? If so, document this wisdom.

2) Using the information from Exercise 1, can you identify specific career-related dreams that may comprise your purpose in service to the world? As you consider the details and requirements of this work, identify energetic blocks that may need healing in order to advance toward your goals.

3) Take some time to evaluate your inner motivations and values as it relates to career. Are you able to shift your energy and perspective toward a more loving (self and others) space for service? Develop a greater understanding of your absolute material needs versus your wants and desires. Along with your alignment to higher values, are you now able to envision a more attainable path to wellness and career fulfillment? Document these findings.

PART I: Affirmations

I AM a spiritual being having a human experience.

I AM now integrating my higher truth into my career pursuits

I AM now focused upon my career as my deeper calling and purpose.

I AM a unique being, able to offer my best gifts and qualities in service to others.

I AM living my unique path for the betterment of all.

I AM now fully capable of living and achieving my highest dreams.

I AM developing greater emotional intelligence, which supports my success.

I AM mindful of my energy, and I heal and grow each day.

I AM in alignment with values that benefit all beings.

I AM consistently offering higher values and service within my career.

I AM successful – loving, fulfilled, abundant, and healthy.

PART II

PROMOTING WELLNESS AND VALUE AT WORK

"I know of no more encouraging fact than the unquestionable ability of man to elevate his life by a conscious endeavor."

- Henry David Thoreau

PART II: Prologue

As you begin to develop a deeper understanding of your purpose and value around career, you become better prepared to contribute more and experience greater fulfillment. You are assimilating your best human qualities with consciousness and the intention to serve. This gives greater meaning and a deeper connection to the work you do each day. As you become aligned with your inner truth, your success becomes more intrinsic, intentional and authentic.

Knowing that your development is ongoing, you will continue to utilize the teaching from Part I. In Part II, it is the application of this wisdom that will support you in maintaining and expressing your healthiest energy and perspective within your specific work conditions. Additionally, your focus on the creation of a healthy work/life balance will further enhance your success and wellness.

Utilizing your mindfulness and presence will facilitate the most empowering work relationships. Learn to promote cooperation and Unity within your work commitments. Create greater efficiency and productivity by managing your time and communications with intention. Connect to the qualities of joy and satisfaction as a way to sustain your passion and bliss. Through inner healing and outer expansion, surpass the self-imposed limits of your vulnerability. And endeavor to focus on the bigger picture of giving and receiving value.

PART II: Energetic Quality or Tool

The energetic quality that I am offering in support of wellness and value at work is **MINDFULNESS**. Within this context, mindfulness supports presence, acceptance, accountability, and focus. We offer our best energy, connected to our deepest truth, while we are mindful. We accept a more empowered identity, and focus on the task at hand without unnecessary distraction or drama. We are more content to simply do our best for its own sake.

The detractor of mindfulness is **DELUSION**. Our delusion, created by our ego-nature and false education, is a barrier to the realization of our truth. In a disconnected state, our mind and energy shifts to fear-based expressions (anxiety, stress, selfishness, blame, etc.). We are no longer creating our best within the reality of the present moment. We instead get lost in the past, future, opinions of others, or some self-defeating belief that distracts from our happiness and the fulfillment of our purpose.

Mindfulness is an energy and activity that empowers you in the present moment. From this place you may find balance and wholeness, efficiency and production, cooperation and Unity, impeccable communication, personal joy and satisfaction, healing, growth, and career fulfillment. While on the enlightened path, your job is to live within this energy, or otherwise re-align to it, as often as possible. **Mindfulness is both a higher quality and spiritual tool.**

CHAPTER 10
Job One: Getting Hired

"No one can discover you until you do. Exploit your talents, strengths and skills and make the world sit up and take notice."

- Rob Liano

A Higher Perspective

You may have previously thought that this is where you begin, on the road to career fulfillment. I will just get hired and then figure it out from there. This mentality says, "A job is a job, I just need to pay my bills." And sometimes, this is the position we are in, so we do what we need to do.

However, beyond the temporary needs of survival, I have been describing many other considerations as a preparation to getting your best job and performing your best service. The point of this is to teach the importance of first understanding your unique qualities/qualifications, deeper dreams and purpose, and to define and map your higher potential according to your values. I also taught about the significance of the spiritual and emotional component.

My goal is to guide you to begin to define and prepare yourself for your best career, in alignment with your true Authentic Self. Hopefully you have, or will, embark upon this process of inner connection and assessment. You have faculties within you that are available for guidance and inspiration. To the extent that you intentionally learn your inner truth by regularly connecting within, you have a significant advantage as you proceed along your enlightened career path.

This becomes the difference between just accepting what comes, and creating your own destiny. Are you going to grope through the darkness of chaotic or "random" experience in order to find your inner truth? Ultimately you may get there, but the journey is often arduous and perilous.

And the truth is that you are likely defining your level of satisfaction based upon how others treat you or recognize your value. If we are wise, we learn that this is our job and not their responsibility. Our deeper energetic involvement is always the best approach.

So here you are, looking for someone to hire you. Whether this is your first job, a new job, or even a new client or customer, you are to express your energy in the most effective way in order to achieve your goal. Sometimes this process is remarkably easy. I have been offered jobs in the past without looking for one; right place – right time. And I have experienced periods of months, unemployed and looking for work. So this is not an exact science.

I say that "getting hired" is Job One because it is the initial step leading directly toward expressing your energy and outer service within your work setting. If you have already done the inner work, you should have a better idea as to your motivations, willingness, and passion for committing to your work. Yet, this does not automatically make the job you are pursuing a "good" job, or the "right" job. You will continue the process of discovery, as more information is revealed to your awareness. And, you will interact with people to learn about the intentions and values of the company.

Otherwise, what many people do is offer a false show of their best qualities (and words) in order to deceive someone into hiring them. Their inner motivations are aligned with ego/fear – what they can get from this job, instead of what they can contribute. They may in fact get hired, according to the delusion, desperation, or apathy of the interviewer. Yet, ultimately your job performance will be consistent with your inner motivations. In this case, lower values equal low quality, effort, and satisfaction. True fulfillment requires that you authentically offer your best energy and intentions in your work.

As you honor yourself, you are positioned within the greatest potential for fulfillment. This not only relates to being hired, but also as the framework of a deeper connection and alignment with the job. This is because your focus and energy for receiving and accepting this job offer, are consistent with the energy of successfully performing the job. You are authentic throughout this process.

Now, even if you are not offered this specific job, strive to retain your highest outlook and intentions. You have not lost value; you simply weren't the best match for this job. Maintain your inner-strength and self-love and move onto the next opportunity. Life is a process in which we may always learn, heal, grow, and ascend. It is your inner awareness and expressions of love that matter most.

Pursuit of Employment

Getting hired depends upon the occurrence of two things: one, a job offer, and two, an acceptance. A job offer is based on several factors. First, that the job you are interested in is available. This begins with your effort to identify an opening by exhausting all of the avenues at your disposal. You may search on-line job sites, employment agencies, personal contacts, or simply walk into a company of interest and ask if they are hiring.

Next, you hold a firm belief that your skills and qualifications matchup to the desires of the prospective employer. Finally, when you find an opening for the job in which you feel qualified and passionate about, you must receive and then navigate the job interview.

Of course, this can be a very challenging process, which takes great effort, skill, patience, and self-belief. All the more reason to pursue the work that is most connected to your gifts, skills, interests, passion, and purpose. Exhibiting your authentic presence is your best tool for connecting to the interviewer in pursuit of your best work opportunity.

In some places the jobs are not so readily available, so you must be prepared to realistically address this situation. Therefore, you may need to be open to learning a new skill, go where the work is more plentiful, or temporarily accept whatever work is available. Yet, always endeavor to do your best and offer your integrity in whatever you do. Limitations need only be temporary, and life is a process. Focus upon your work as your potential for contribution, and remain open to situations and opportunities that lead to fulfillment.

Before applying for a job, as best you can, evaluate the employment details, as well as the prospective employer. This is a combination of external and internal input. Continue to do the inner work to best define your dreams, values, and purpose. Prepare yourself with your best energy (self-love, self-confidence, self-worth, etc.), knowing that you are pursuing something that not only supports you materially, but also aligns with your unique path and presence.

The Interview

Now, you have been given an opportunity to participate in an interview for a job that seems desirable. Be prepared to discuss your skills and qualities with honest enthusiasm.

While honoring your truth, express your joy for offering your best contribution to the company, and support to your co-workers. This connects you with your interviewer on a deeper level, and displays higher emotional intelligence. By far, most interviewers will appreciate a positive attitude, perspective, enthusiasm, and caring, over someone with extreme skill or intelligence that lacks empathy and humility.

You are each spiritual beings having a human experience. In this moment each of you are attempting to fulfill a purpose in the most beneficial way. You want a good job, and the interviewer wants to hire a good employee. And you need each other in order to satisfactorily accomplish your goals. Therefore, show respect, caring, compassion, and on the level of energy – love.

Your best authentic energy and attitude should help set you apart from other candidates; energetically you are leading with integrity, and this can be sensed by others. This will at least offer the interviewer an opportunity to consider you within the perspective of your best light. Now, even if they choose to go in a different direction, at least you can accept that this was about them; your best job is still out there.

The Job Offer

Congratulations, you have been offered the job! Now, you need to decide whether or not to accept. But, before you do, consider the following.

What were your observations about the company when on-site? How do you connect on the level of energy to the interviewer, especially if they are going to be your boss? Do you feel inspired or defeated before you even start? Based upon the expectations expressed in the interview, how does this work line up with your interests and skillset? Is the initial compensation satisfactory? What is this job to you – a step toward your best career, or simply a job that will help support you through your further development, leading to your best career?

If possible, ask for a brief (but specific) period of time to consider the offer. Meditate on this situation. What inner messages or guidance are you receiving about this job offer? What is your "gut" or intuition telling you? Is there excitement, even in the face of vulnerability for the unknown? Or do you feel dread, and see only "red flags" warning you to keep searching?

This is your career opportunity, so be accountable for your process, and honor your truth. When we feel fearful within, we are more likely to experience desperation. Admittedly, there are times when we believe that our options are minimal, and we may feel required to accept any job. Yet, whenever possible identify with your higher truth and utilize the inner preparation that you have developed. Always do your best to put yourself in work situations that are more connected to your truth and supportive of your highest career fulfillment.

CHAPTER 11
Job Two: Work Performance

"Out of the current confusion of ideals and confounding of career hopes, a calm recognition may yet emerge that productive labor is the foundation of all prosperity."

- Mathew B. Crawford

Inner Wellness Leads to High Performance

Congratulations, you got the job! Now it is time to do the work. Performance is *HOW* you do your work; this is about both the process AND results. Are you engaged with your best energy and effort? Are you focused on doing your best within your level of skill and ability? Is your inner motivation guiding you toward high performance, as your definition of success? Do you have a deep caring about how your co-workers, customers, and outside associates are impacted by your work? High performance requires "yes" answers to all.

These are all internal qualities, which is why I spent some effort teaching the value of inner preparation in Part I. Are there external issues that may impact your performance – yes, of course. However, personal growth and wellness is about focusing upon the aspects of life in which you have the greatest control. And, as it turns out, this will have the greatest impact on your healthy perspective and the quality of your work performance.

Some of the outside concerns may be positively impacted by your attitude, intentions, and efforts, while other issues will remain beyond your direct influence for change. Yet, your best inner-strength and self-love will support you in minimizing negative external situations. You will more readily accept "what is" – and then choose to heal, grow, and make the best of it. It will also lead you to honoring yourself without the need to dishonor others.

However, as discussed in Part I, it is your inner perceptions and expressions of energy (i.e. Self-Mastery) that give you the authority to experience your life in the most enlightened and empowering way. As it relates to Career Fulfillment, a key factor is in the degree to which your work choices are aligned with your Authentic Self. In other words, when we are severally out of alignment and disconnected from our truth while attempting to perform our job, we will face internal conflict that is unsupportive to our best performance and well-being.

At this point, you are fighting against the current of your best loving energy. In this case, not only are you trying to deal with outside challenges, but you are also fighting yourself. This is ultimately a losing battle. Instead of honoring your truth, your inner motivation becomes – trying to control external situations merely to survive and retain your job or income.

This is a struggle that many people routinely face. As humans we are quite resilient when we need be, so we can continue to function for a time under these conditions. But the truth is that we are not performing at our best. And we are unable to create sufficient enthusiasm, interest, and passion for the job. Therefore, there is little, if any, fulfillment.

While in this very uncomfortable space, you may be unaware of a better path. You lose connection to your Spirit and simply go through the motions. This is uninspiring to all involved, and unsupportive to your fulfillment or the success of your employer. Within your holistic existence, this negativity bleeds into the other aspects of your life. Hopefully, all of this will be evidence of your need to awaken and change your course. You must find a way to elevate your consciousness and perceive a higher path for your life and work. You need to re-connect to your Spirit or Authentic Self.

Integrating Your Humanity and Spirituality

Our best job performance utilizes both our unique human qualities as well as our higher spiritual capacity. You may not have previously thought of your job performance using this terminology. This is not about religion, tradition, or beliefs; this involves the application of your inner power and truth. You have an inner light that needs to be switched on, in order to give optimal performance and receive your highest benefit. This is the enlightened path that supports career fulfillment.

As a part of your accountability for your best life, you are charged with the responsibility of assessing your career path through your ongoing mindfulness. Are you presently performing at your best level? Or do you need to focus on some inner healing that supports a re-connection to your truth. Endeavor to elevate your energy to the higher expressions of love within your current job.

Sometimes the problem is not the job (boss, co-workers, compensation, etc.), and instead, you have created your own problems internally. For whatever reason (and life offers us many) you have abandoned your own self-love, mindfulness, and accountability for creating your most empowered life. It then becomes an easy trap to just blame others, life, God, or whomever, for your dissatisfaction.

At other times, your life/work assessment will conclude that this job is not presently in alignment with your true passion and purpose. Not only that, but continuing to function in this work will further distance you from your achievement of career fulfillment. You may decide that honoring your truth must lead you in a new direction. Now you utilize your best internal and external analysis and intuition in order to devise an empowering plan to move forward.

Within the state of high performance you are intentionally and continually in the right place at the right time. This is not a fluke, coincidence, or happenstance, but instead, it is alignment with your Authentic Self. Consequently, you must maintain this internally generated state that honors your wisdom (connection to your deeper truth), mindfulness (intention and focus within each present moment), and accountability (willingness to claim responsibility for all that you create/experience).

Even if you utilize a different language to describe this deeper process, these principles are designed to authorize, support, and empower you to realize your greatest success at work. Your highest level of performance is unattainable, or at least unsustainable, without a connection to your inner love, value, worth, peace, and joy. However, when motivated toward inner wellness and truth, your intentions and effort at work are aligned with these Divine qualities. Accordingly, you will create success and fulfill a deeper purpose in the performance of your job.

The remainder of Part II is dedicated to integrating your greater inner qualities and wisdom within various external work related issues. You will learn some of the tools and higher perceptions that create more optimal and advantageous conditions and relationships in support of the success for all involved. As you have noticed, my view of success requires that you work/develop from the inside out. It is the promotion of your inner wellness and best qualities that leads to offering your greatest value and contribution at work – this is Career Fulfillment.

CHAPTER 12
Enhancing Life Balance

"I've learned that making a 'living' is not the same thing as 'making a life'."

- Maya Angelou

What is Life Balance?

For most people, this "mythical creature" is hard to define, and even harder to maintain. Everyone manages their life the best they know how. Maybe we can all do better.

Within all aspects of our life we have various responsibilities and opportunities. We are responsible for our health and wellness, for work that supports our needs for fulfillment and sustenance, as well as time for fun, rest and recovery. We are also responsible for our commitments to certain other people. The amount of time and effort involved in each of these areas will be different for everyone. Yet, we must be intentional and self-disciplined in order to balance these things successfully.

With a new education and perspective, you might be empowered to more often honor your higher values and live empowered. The principles of enlightenment utilize the wisdom, mindfulness, and accountability that will support your present moment choices to consciously include inner and outer wellness. With greater consciousness you will enhance your life balance, and the overall quality of your life.

Otherwise, we tend to diminish this quality and balance. Through fear and delusion we may over prioritize our involvement in things that are less supportive to our well-being. We may waste our time and then be hurried and anxious, or we will involve ourselves in things that undermine our own wellness.

At times you will naturally be required to focus more energy into certain aspects or circumstances over others. And you may feel overly burdened and challenged. It may feel like the "choice" for balance is not available. However, this should be a temporary situation and not the norm.

Your awareness should notice when your energy is being depleted to your detriment. And then it will be up to you to change, heal, and re-align in some way. As hectic as life can be, self-mastery is a key to sustained balance and success.

The real truth is that we typically find the time and make the greatest effort toward the things that are most important to us. Therefore, your first priority is to elevate your consciousness and align with your higher truth and healthy values. This is most supportive to you on a holistic level. And secondly, you may further develop better time management skills.

If you are feeling overwhelmingly stressed-out, dissatisfied, and disempowered, you must choose to awaken. Be responsible for resolving your issues (healing your energy), and shifting your behavior (energetic expressions). To do otherwise, is evidence of your choice to remain stuck in the conditions from which you perceive your suffering.

Applying Greater Wisdom

When you are out of balance, overemphasizing certain aspects of life while ignoring others, you may be expending your energy in an unsustainable way. Worse yet, is when this imbalance is applied to activities or things that are destructive or unsupportive to your wellness. An honest assessment of your usage of time, mental framework, and inner motivations will reveal a need for you to apply wisdom, mindfulness, and accountability.

We think that because of our lack of productivity or satisfaction there is not enough time, yet, this is only a symptom of the real inner problems. Maybe you are spending too much energy toward work – not enough for relationships/rest/play (or vice versa). Is this work fulfilling, rewarding, and serving your deeper love, joy, peace, and wellness?

If it is fulfilling, then you are likely not experiencing disempowerment and suffering. If it is not fulfilling, then why is this job such a priority over your own wellness? Are you doing the wrong job or the right job in the wrong way? And if you are creating an imbalance by avoiding or de-emphasizing your career, why are you not seeking fulfillment within this endeavor?

We may be overloading an aspect of giving or receiving (work or otherwise) that will bring an overall depletion of energetic health and wellness – whether physical, mental, emotional, or spiritual. Therefore, assess your life and determine where you need to heal and shift your perspective and energetic expressions toward a greater alignment with your authentic truth.

Only you can be accountable for this. Even with the usual outside influences and pressure that exists from time to time, the sooner you become responsible for assessing, accepting, and supporting your needs, the better your life will be. This is a choice to enhance life balance and live more enlightened.

If you are presently attached to people who discourage or hinder your ability to properly choose wellness and balance for yourself, you must be empowered for change. First, become fully aware of your situation, which may entail accepting accountability for all that you have created – without shame or self-judgment.

Next, you may need to focus on elevating your own self-love and self-worth. Know that you are enough, and worthy of your own happy, fulfilled life. Connected to your true identity, this is your purpose.

Finally, access your inner courage and strength to claim your power of choice in the present moment. You cannot change the past, so work toward a "re-boot" of the present. This need not condemn or vilify anyone else; your demonstration of personal healing and growth is solely for the sake of your own well-being.

A common issue that makes life balance a challenge comes in our partner or family relationships. There is a balance between caring for others and caring for ourselves. Sometimes we may be so focused on helping others that we undermine our own well-being. We are judging our commitment through guilt or some other aspect of fear.

This is not only detrimental to us, but, more often than not, we are robbing the other person of finding their power and fulfilling their own needs and purpose. When we can be more grounded in loving energy, we will honor ourselves and recognize others as having value and authority over their live.

Another kind of imbalance is determined by the quality of our energetic expressions. As we are integrating our Divinity into our humanity, we are balancing the energy of love against that of ego/fear. Therefore, we must be able to notice when our thoughts are too routinely negative – either against ourselves or others. We may be overwhelming our loving energy with the preponderance of energetic expressions stuck in the lower energy of ego. In this case, even if our activities are relatively balanced and healthy, we are out of alignment with our truth and creating our own dissatisfaction and suffering.

Balancing Energy

Our healthy energy flows in a manner that gives and receives as an optimal balance. The responsibility for sustaining an adequate balance is ours alone – no one else can do this for us. Unfortunately, we typically will prioritize and address most everything that comes at us from the outside.

Higher wisdom comes in to play regarding our understanding and willingness to care for our own energetic wellness first. With mindfulness we may monitor and manage the impact of our own exertion and our need to replenish or heal. The way in which we engage others and the frequency of engagement are within your power to control (to a large degree). This is a formula that we each must determine for ourselves. This is why I always emphasize the need for you to connect with your Authentic Self, to understand and evaluate your unique qualities, needs, and desires.

Some people have an energetic capacity that exceeds that of others. You must learn how far and hard to drive yourself before you create destructive conditions. You can notice when you need to back off, to heal and restore.

Know your limits and be mindful of your energy levels. Transcend the ego-education that tells you it is weak to slow down, rest, and heal – this is pure ignorance. And it is foolish to allow yourself to be judged and bullied by others when you know it is in your best interest to listen to your truth.

You will certainly compete and achieve at your best when in alignment with your Authentic Self. You are applying your balanced loving energy, and your achievements represent inner goals that are fulfilling for you. When you try to be like someone else, or are motivated by their judgements to your detriment, you are not honoring yourself. This leads to imbalance, dissatisfaction, and even poor health.

Another consideration, from the standpoint of enlightenment, is to honor other people. Your energy is different than theirs, and vice versa. They may have issues (health or otherwise) that you are unaware of. Therefore, never admonish or criticize those who function on a level different than you. Learn to be compassionate and supportive of others, while living your own truth.

Wisdom directs us to learn and trust our own truth, monitor our energy through mindfulness, and determine our own goals for achievement and fulfillment. In living this way, you will find many occasions that will challenge your false training of what "should be." And people will "show up" to remind you of these expectations.

On the level of energy you are attracting them in order to reflect back to you your own disempowering beliefs. It takes great awareness and courage to follow your truth and live within your healthiest energetic flow. To the extent you do, set your own boundaries, as it relates to balance within your unique life path.

Higher Values Support Life Balance

I previously spoke about the significance of claiming higher values (Chapter 9). In order to be in alignment with your deeper truth you must live within the higher values that intrinsically lead to success and wellness for you. And this is also relevant with regard to enhancing your life balance.

Are you overemphasizing thoughts and activities that represent lower values - primarily ego-driven? You should know what this means by now. Are you even considering that which is more meaningful and intrinsically supportive to your wellness and enjoyment of life? Do you simply "run out of daylight," trying to fit way too much into your daily life? What is your motivation and expectation for your level of productivity? It is the priority of your values that establish what is most important for you to focus on each day. Then from there, all you can do is your best.

To emphasize the expression of your energy and effort toward activities that are directed to "manipulating or getting ahead of others" or "maximizing your income or prestige," are values to be sure. While they likely fit into the desires of nearly all humans, under the influence of ego, they do not directly satisfy us on the deeper levels of love, joy, peace, fulfillment, and holistic wellness. Once again, there is a balance to be determined within your values. There is a price to pay for expressing your energy in ways that lead to imbalance.

We cannot overemphasize our egocentric work pursuits and expect fulfillment on a spiritual level – which is our primary identity. We cannot overly tax the physical body and not expect that it will breakdown in some capacity. We cannot absorb or express great negativity with other people, and not be detrimentally impacted mentally or emotionally. So if we continue to push ourselves in ways that disregard the inner energetic signs and causes of wellness, we are choosing to experience suffering.

Wisdom supports us in understanding the benefit of pursuing both our spiritual and material needs and desires. Therefore, if you feel you are lacking in any particular area, you may need to re-prioritize your values. Do you need to change a behavior or do you need to elevate your perceptions? This is the more holistic view of your life that leads to deeper success and fulfillment.

To the extent that you express great unhappiness about your pace of life, or in all of the tasks that you do not complete, you will need to make some changes in order to experience more peace and satisfaction. This is always up to you. Sometimes we are more comfortable within the familiar stress and chaos that we have always created. Personal growth leads to self-mastery and wellness, which is quite relevant to life balance issues. But more than anything, personal accountability, intention, and effort are required.

Firstly, you must learn to release your idea of perfectionism. Your efforts to satisfy everyone around you, including your own lofty expectations, are unfounded in truth. By your very nature you are setting yourself up for failure. Do not condemn yourself or prostrate yourself to others while doing your best and aligned with your higher values. Regardless of your upbringing and ego training, you are not here to be perfect, or meet the unreasonable standards of anyone else. You are here to determine your inner truth and then do your best to honor it.

With an understanding of your truth and values you may need the courage to accept yourself and create healthy boundaries with others. This will likely be a process. In learning to say "no" to other people, your best tool is firm but empathetic communication. If others have always relied upon you, or have taken advantage of you, then this change may be jolting to them. In truth, this can be supportive as a reminder to them that they are capable and primarily responsible for themselves.

The bottom line is that you are taking back your power, but it must not come from a place of anger or fear. Find great inner peace in this declaration of self-love and empowerment. You are choosing to honor yourself on a deeper level, so express your energy from this place of love.

In truth, our blaming others, seeking perfection, or being more comfortable in our own dysfunction are expressions of our own delusion. However, not to be unkind, but as often as not, this is about our own laziness or indifference. Lazy thinking looks for the easiest way out. Enlightenment requires our best effort and intention for inner healing and growth. This means being accountable for our own wellness, without the need to diminish others. If we are unwilling to do this then we have only ourselves to blame.

Career Fulfillment

Enhance your life balance by scheduling your time and expectations in a way that is more healthy, reasonable, and attainable. This includes activities in support of others as well as honoring your need for rest, healing, and enjoyment. You may also benefit from better time management tools (discussed later), yet the initial phase of change will come from the application of wisdom and your commitment to self-love and higher values.

Creating Time to Disconnect from Work

Work, work, and more work. For all of you workaholics, here's some good news – with technology you can now be connected to work 24/7! Oh wait, that's potentially dreadful news. Now, more than ever, we must develop the wisdom, mindfulness, and personal accountability to monitor and manage our expressions of energy – our inner wellness – regarding our time commitment to our jobs.

It comes down to your priorities and values. Is your focus for fulfillment: happiness, wellness, and abundance (in all of its forms)? Or is it status, approval, and monetary concerns. Even if you are all-in on higher contribution in service to the world, you need to create the space and time to temporarily disconnect from work.

There exists a balance that supports both your holistic wellness and your best effort in your career. It is not for me or anyone else to determination the specifics, as only you can know your inner truth. And within the teaching in this book I am always promoting that you utilize your higher awareness to read the signs of distress before they devastate your health and mental/emotional well-being. With a consistent connection to awareness you may establish the general guidelines and boundaries that are most supportive for you.

Again, depending upon your job duties and responsibilities you may or may not feel pressure to sacrifice your life balance in order to succeed. Within some professions there is certainly a trade-off. Often times, more responsibility leads to more commitment and effort, which potentially leads to greater income. Self-employed is another scenario where a great time commitment is often required, even while you may enjoy more freedom.

So you may be in a position where you feel that you must work a great number of hours per day/week in order to enhance your income or freedom – i.e. trade-off. The greatest point here is to "live consciously." In other words, be mindful of the benefits and the sacrifices as best you can.

From this energetic space, choose the path that aligns with your inner truth. This is YOUR choice, so claim the joy and peace within this decision. If you cannot live in joy or peace, make another choice.

For whatever your situation, setup the boundaries and practices that support you in fulfilling your work obligations, while still tending to your personal needs. With our "smart" phones and other computer devices we are susceptible to work overload and distraction any time of the day or night. Therefore, learn to disconnect from these things in order to actually experience "personal time" away from work thoughts or activities. Create a work-free zone of time per day or week, simply to release work related stress and to support holistic wellness and joy. This will greatly enhance the expression of your best energy when you are fully engaged in your job.

This is not just a "work" thing. As society has become so habitually connected to their devices, even much of our personal time can be wasted in the countless mind-numbing apps, games, and social media platforms. Better to actually live your life, according to your unique gifts, purpose, and path, than to "follow" people you don't really know, or be overly concerned about posting every little thing you do or experience. Find the intrinsic value of living your own life, for your own benefit. And "share" your life and energy with the real people that you are actually connected to, like your partner, children, family, friends, and co-workers.

Balance Enhancing Tools

In determining and adjusting to a healthier balance for you, you may benefit from some empowering practices. Even though we are spiritual beings having a human experience, it does not make this human experience any less demanding on many levels. While our Spirit exists beyond time and space, our humanity requires our constant attention here and now, merely for survival.

So when I talk about integration and balance, I am speaking about the benefit of interceding with greater awareness and loving qualities into your human challenges. The majority of your focus and time will be devoted to your work – which supports your material well-being. Therefore, it is crucial that you approach your career from a higher perspective.

What you do for work and how you do it is vitally important toward sustaining overall energetic wellness. So even if you spend 50 hours a week involved in your job, when mindful and aligned with purpose, your work may be energizing. Additionally, in your non-work related hours, you will still need to create and support healing and wellness.

There are two main keys to holistic healing and energizing during this available time. The first is being fully present in what you are doing. And second, is to develop habits and practices that directly support your wellness.

Regardless of what you are doing, be present and mindful. Whether you are at work, or spending time with family or friends, doing chores, caring for your body, etc., maintain a mental focus on the task at hand. Living in the moment is more than a cliché. Your power lives within this state of consciousness. This is because you are placing your energy more exclusively in the only time that ever exists – the present.

When you are doing one thing (or multiple things) your brain is bouncing back and forth and your attention and energy is divided and weakened. Even if these activities are relatively positive and beneficial individually, your best power is not being utilized. You are draining yourself with less than optimal results. This is both unsatisfying and unproductive.

Worse yet is when our attention vacillates between the past and the future, while we are hoping to live our best life in the present. For the most part, the past holds us to memories that are unsatisfying judgments involving our prior selves. And our preoccupation with the future keeps us feeling anxious of the unknowable. When this occurs, you are not balanced and grounded in the present moment. Plus, you are not as effectively completing the task at hand.

Success in this area is largely a matter of mental discipline and practice, in that, with your growing awareness you will at least be able to realize when your thoughts or activities are not supporting your wellness or productivity. This is a great time to both incorporate your higher values and slow down to re-focus. Maintain a connection to your breath, which always exists in the present moment. And otherwise return to your breath as often as needed.

Next, prioritize that which is most supportive, while letting go of unnecessary burdens. Some things we can either eliminate or defer to a better time and space. Therefore, endeavor to stay present and do your best in all that you do.

As for choosing healthy practices, you want to create the space to promote "being" – which connects you to your Spirit. The best practice of which I am aware is meditation and prayer. You take a few moments to release your normal thinking, planning, and physical doing, in an environment free from the distraction of other people.

This is a great reminder of your true identity and life force. It only takes a few focused minutes a day, but is invaluable for re-setting your deeper connection to truth. Meditation is something you do purely for your own wellness; though it is supportive of the higher nature and consciousness with all beings.

Other healthy practices will either directly support the health of your physical body, or involve "doing" simply for the enjoyment of it. To the extent that you are capable, physical exercise is a valuable way to enhance your wellness and bring balance to your life. Although there are countless jobs and work settings, many jobs these days involve sitting in front of a computer all day. As individuals and as a society many of us have developed very sedentary lifestyles. And on top of that, our typical diets contain foods that feed our addictions (sugar, fat, salt, chemicals, etc.) instead of the health of our body.

In addition to adequate exercise and a proper diet, two other health factors are hydration and sleep. In the next book in the series I will go into great deal about – *Holistic Wellness*. In the meantime, drinking a sufficient amount of clean water is vital to the health of the physical body and supports many of its systems. As far as an adequate amount of sleep, just know that most people do not get enough of it in order to function optimally in their lives. If you need more, structure your life to get more. As always, if you have medical questions about any of these topics, please consult your physician.

It is more important than ever before to intentionally create habits and practices that are designed to directly support your wellness. Within the context of this Chapter about Life Balance, and this book about Career Fulfillment, I am addressing the holistic nature of your life and the role it plays in your success and wellness.

Now, in relation to the level of stress or imbalance coming from your work, you may determine the time and effort needed toward these healthy practices. I have heard it said, "If you do not have the time to meditate once per day, you should be meditating twice." Of course, many people who function in this way will keep going until they breakdown (in one form or another).

This is a choice that you must make for yourself. My hope is that you will live more enlightened and choose a healthier path for your life. In this way you will intervene on your own behalf by choosing to shift your behavior before a breakdown is necessary. With mindfulness you will recognize the warning signs and heed their message.

Our energy (within all of our body systems) is self-regulating. It operates on a much higher frequency and capacity than our ego nature. While this may seem like an inconvenience to you when you think you "need" to get things done, it is a built-in protection to keep you alive and to support your evolution. When you neglect your own holistic wellness there are consequences.

On the level of energy, balance is a spiritual principle. It not only helps sustain your human life, it also guides you to greater effectiveness and efficiency within the fulfillment and achievement of your career and non-career goals. All of this represents an enlightened approach toward creating and maintaining career fulfillment.

CHAPTER 13
Time Management Considerations

*"The bad news is that time flies.
The good news is that you are the pilot."*

- Michael Altshuler

Energy Management

Your goal is to maximize wellness and value in your work and life; this requires the balancing of energy. As you now know, your energy gets expressed in the ways that you typically process as human – as your thoughts, words, feelings, and actions. This leads you into all of the various activities and interactions that consume your day, and eventually your life.

You may call this balancing of energy and functions – Time Management. Yet, this is a bit of a misnomer, as time moves independent of your intentions, desires, or effort. You cannot manage time itself, but you can attempt to manage how you use your time in each present moment.

Adequate time management must reflect a higher quality of energetic wellness. In this way, your productivity is most effective in ways that are supportive to you. This incorporates both your spiritual and human qualities and considerations. And it not only impacts career fulfillment, but also your life as a whole. Once again, I am taking a holistic perspective for the benefit of work and life.

Four keys to improving your Time Management:

- You must first become aware of how you spend your time. *Awareness* is the first step in transformation.

- You must decide what is most important relating to your values. Connecting to your *higher values* will help release you from your ego-driven distractions.

- You must be *accountable* for shifting and elevating your behavior through discipline, intention, and healthy practices.

- And you must be *mindful* and focused in the present moment, in order to maintain the most effective use of your time.

While "Time Management" is an accepted secular term, in truth, this sounds like a spiritual process to me. It is about elevating the quality and expressions of your energy. In other words, it is more about your inner approach and accountability than it is about external tools or excuses.

The way in which you organize and structure your life and activities will be a factor in the successful management of your time. However, there are other considerations on the enlightened path that are more relevant and supportive to you.

In the following sections of this Chapter I will discuss: The Importance of Mindfulness; Shifting your Energy and Intentions; Setting Appropriate Goals/Expectations; and Honoring your Commitments.

The Importance of Mindfulness

The overriding spiritual practice in support of quality Time Management is Mindfulness. Where is my energy in

Career Fulfillment

this present moment? What is required of me in order to successfully complete this task? What is my deeper purpose or value in performing this task? How do I stay present and focused throughout this task?

As you desire to evaluate your effectiveness, are you even aware of how you express your energy (moment-to-moment, hourly, daily, etc.)? When you are working, you may primarily function in one of four ways. 1) You are conscious of your inner thoughts and external words and actions in a given moment; you are focused and connected to the task at hand. 2) You are taking up physical space in the present, but your mind is lost in some pointless side track, past experience, or day dream about the future. 3) You are relatively unconscious or unintentional as you simply react to the energy around you – you are on "ego-autopilot." Or 4) you are basically overwhelmed, disappointed in yourself, and fearful that you will never get organized or "caught up." This leads to some level of anxiety and stress; both unproductive and unfulfilling.

First of all, move past judgement, this is not a matter of "good or bad," this simply relates to your current mental framework. Yet, with training, focus, and practice you can transform your limitations and improve your effectiveness. In order to manage your time in the most constructive and beneficial way you must be connected to the present moment. Of what value are lists of to-do items if you cannot be present, and focus your energy upon the current task?

Additionally, even with present moment focus, if you expect to satisfactorily complete a task, you must allow a reasonable time frame for this job. By "reasonable" I mean that YOU are able to perform it. This takes into consideration your energy, other commitments, personality, talents, etc.

If the demands you are working under are excessive for you, whether or not they come from other people, you must honestly assess the situation and make some adjustment.

Remember, the highest standard is always to do your best. So, you must find a way to be satisfied while honoring your best.

At times you need to express an uncomfortable truth to another person in order to redefine expectations. You may need to ask for help, or otherwise, admit that this is something that you are presently unable to do. At other times, you will be required to pull time away from some other activity. In any case, be accountable for your energy and well-being.

As you move through your day, there is time for intense focus, and time for allowing your mind to wander and wonder. After all, you are not a robot. *The effectiveness of your time management comes in knowing which is most appropriate in any given moment, and this requires mindfulness.*

Training in mindfulness is a matter of practice. Through your intentions you may gradually become more often aware of the present. You will notice your breath, and through your presence, when you witness mental distraction, fear, or anxiety, you can stay fixed upon your breath for a few extra moments. This supports you in being more grounded in reality, instead of continually floating away to the next memory or non-constructive thought.

You may learn to realize and experience the present moment as powerful, healing, and supportive. You can only realize the existence of your Spirit in these moments. Otherwise, you waste your only real opportunity to accomplish what you most desire.

Mindfulness is the key to connecting to your truth and power. From there, it is up to you to define the most beneficial and essential activities to be accomplished in any given time frame. Only you can make this determination. Use your inner strength and wisdom to connect to higher values, and then choose to honor your best path.

Just as importantly, be kind and compassionate to yourself. Growth and transformation are a gradual and ongoing process. Your goal is to do your best – not to experience perfection. The biggest waste of time comes from self-defeating judgments or criticism of yourself and other people. Always remember, the more loving and compassionate we are with ourselves the more we will express this energy to all others. And everybody wins.

Shifting your Energy and Intentions

The quality of the energy you bring into a situation impacts the experience, for better or worse. The greatest determinant of career success would be in contributing your best to a job that routinely fulfills a deeper purpose and connects to your higher truth. Therefore, as a primary goal, your ideal career would involve a job where the vast majority of tasks are intrinsically fulfilling and purposeful. On the enlightened path you will use wisdom, mindfulness, and accountability to eventually align your career in this way.

Have you noticed that you have a way of making time for the things that are most meaningful or satisfying to you? This is true for all people. Yet, you must be careful not to equate meaningful with easy or gentle to your ego.

We tend to prioritize or emphasize the things we enjoy doing, at the expense of that which is less pleasant. This could be in the performance of a specific chore or in dealing with certain other individuals that you find difficult. Some things naturally connect to our inner bliss, while other things awaken our inner fear. So how do we shift our energy to recognize value in all of the tasks we endeavor to undertake?

If your current task easily connects you to your bliss, then you are already there. Very little effort is required to do this thing with great interest and passion. You are committing your best energy to this task, and finding enjoyment in the process. You are said to be, "in the flow." Is there any wonder that you will recognize success in this situation? In fact, in this example you will more easily claim your success without the need for confirmation or approval from others. For me this happens when I am writing.

Yet, even in your best career there are aspects and occasions where you must fulfill a task that is in some way more challenging or difficult for you. This is where your intention toward mindfulness is most valuable regarding the management of your time. Are you losing focus while dreading this task, and therefore, putting it off or delaying the inevitable?

If so, you are allowing your presence to reside in fear, and you are delaying the fulfillment of the task that would bring empowerment. Plus, you are disrupting your overall schedule of tasks. Sometimes you are required to perform a duty that is unpleasant or contrary to your best skillset, or one that simply comes at a time when your energy feels depleted. This is the reality of work.

If this task is a requirement of your job (or otherwise necessary), use your present moment power to overcome your inner fear and doubt. Rather than focusing on your objections to the task, place your energy and intention upon the joy and satisfaction in its completion. Perform to the best of your ability, without the expectation of perfection. It's not that you are seeking out these situations; however, you cannot avoid them and still persist with your personal healing, growth, and ascension. As you conquer these inner demons, you will be amazed at your progress and development.

If this task is not actually required at this time (or at all) you must develop the inner strength to release this unnecessary mental burden. Through your greater presence you are empowered to elevate your energy (belief, perspective, self-love, etc.). This requires focus and effort, but more than mere willpower, your intention is to benefit by choosing to shift your energy and identity in relation to this task.

Depending upon the magnitude of the job or task, you can intentionally elevate your view of YOURSELF. On some level within, you have made this aspect of work bigger than your belief in your own ability. Maybe you reasonably assess that this is not "in your wheel house," yet that does not mean that you are incapable or unworthy of high performance.

Therefore, it is this expansion of your identity from ego to Spirit – or connection to your Authentic Self – that is empowering. It's more than just convincing yourself to do something; it is actually acknowledging that this is a task set before you that must be completed in order to fulfill your higher purpose. And there is nothing ever presented to you on your path that is impossible.

So, step into this role with self-confidence and awareness of your power. As always, do your best. You are releasing the fear of needing to be perfect or doing this as well as someone else. You are approaching this task with your best loving energy. Appreciate yourself throughout this process; this is the path of healing, growth, and ascension.

Utilize your mindfulness and present moment power to effectively focus on the deeper value of the task before you, and then shift your energy to support its completion.

Whether this "less-pleasant" task is a part of your to-do list or schedule, or if it more spontaneously develops, you must concentrate on this with your best energy. In doing this, you transcend the energy of fear by replacing it with the energy of love.

In this case, it is about self-love, as you are now trusting and honoring your deeper truth for the greater benefit of your overall wellness and success. You must be even more willing to remove self-judgment in the performance of this task. Give yourself a break, and acknowledge the empowerment involved in doing something less natural or more difficult for you.

This is a way for you to be accountable for all that you create in your life. It is a sign of healing and growth to determine what is necessary, and then changing your mindset from fear to love, in order to offer your best service. More than anything else, this leads to success and fulfillment.

It is certainly reasonable to think that you can shift your energy for one specific task at a time. Remember, with mindfulness you are fully focused on only the present objective. These types of duties are part of the overall process of fulfilling your job, and you are utilizing your best inner power to perform in a successful way. Even if you have an entire day filled with challenges, you may summon your best energy, and shift your perspective to focus on the higher value of service and contribution.

Advancement in any profession is largely determined by how you express your energy within the moments that are most difficult. This sets you apart from the herd. The integration of your elevated energy into these situations will support you toward accomplishing your objectives and then moving forward onto the next task.

Remember, everything is temporary. Whether you perceive it to be a joy or a challenge, each task comes and goes as it is accomplished. Try to take a more objective view, and recognize each task as an opportunity for fulfillment.

This is the nature of things. When we are fearful of a task or situation, it is a reflection of a deeper issue of healing that you must deal with eventually. For the sake of honoring yourself, it is best to understand this fear and take steps now to heal or resolve inner conflicting energy. In this process of healing it helps to determine the source of the fear within you. Does this relate to a past failure or harsh judgment? Or is this negativity related to a lack of self-love, trust, self-worth, etc.? I hope that you can see that the principles of enlightenment are designed to eradicate this fear and negativity.

Instead of looking upon this as an experience leading to learning and growth, your ego is preventing you from simply trying your best; under the guise of self-protection. The other potential issue is that this work (job or task) is simply not in alignment with your gifts, qualities, interest, and passion. If this is the case, you must consider the appropriateness of the job for you.

Otherwise, to simply ignore the message that your experience is designed to teach you is to dishonor your inner truth, and is a choice to endure suffering in some form. This becomes a drain and distraction that eventually corrupts your overall outlook about yourself, this line of work, and your employer. Even the parts of the job you do well will suffer because your focus is naturally drawn to the thing you fear.

This is how the energy of ego works. It is like a cancer that expands your inner fear and depletes the positive energy. It must be eradicated through the application of higher principles for the sake of healing.

If you decide that this is the work that you want to continue to perform, and that there are certain tasks which require an amount of healing and shifting of energy, then you absolutely have the power to transcend and transform. You may be required to pursue additional training, gain the assistance of others, or make other alterations. However, the initial shift is in recognizing your higher identity and the inner value in performing this task well, which is leading to your growth and success.

You now may focus your best energy and intentions into this specific task. And by doing so, your energy and effort will find a way to complete it to the best of your ability. Even if not perfectly done, there is satisfaction in overcoming your fear and in demonstrating your willingness take on new challenges. This is called growth.

For the sake of healing, growth, and evolution you must face your vulnerability. It is this transcendence that creates your best contribution and fulfillment. Through mindfulness you may become aware of your most appropriate balance. Some will thrive on greater or more frequent challenges than others. However, we cease to grow when we decline or avoid all challenges. We stagnate and our energy becomes more encased in fear.

Therefore, your mindfulness is not only beneficial toward better time management, but also as a tool to guide you through your experiences. Always focus your best energy upon the task at hand. How you connect with deeper value to the very tasks you perform on a daily basis will offer great information of a spiritual and human nature.

From either your relative struggles or preferences you may learn facets of your inner truth, and your best ways to contribute value into the world. Seek the best balance of wellness, challenge, growth, and achievement for you. This will keep you interested and passionate as a way of maintaining greater productivity and effectiveness within your time at work.

Setting Appropriate Goals/Expectations

A proper focus upon your current tasks with mindfulness and purpose is essential. Yet, what is it that you are attempting to complete, produce, or achieve? What is an appropriate goal regarding the most effective use of your time? When should you push through the challenges and when do you take a break and regain your best energy? Do these tasks bring a sense of fulfillment, peace, and satisfaction, or futility, pressure, and anxiety?

Of course, no one can rightfully tell you what you should or shouldn't be doing with your time. But answer these questions: Are you fully satisfied with how you use the time you have? Are you as effective and efficient as you wish to be? And, do you think that it is within your power to improve your time management? If the answer to any or all of these questions is "no," then you might rethink the appropriateness of your goals and expectations.

When I use the term goals, in this context, I am talking about your to-do lists or the volume and type of tasks that you feel you must fulfill in your daily life. Again, "appropriateness" is to be determined by you, according to your unique gifts, qualities, interests, passion, and purpose.

The key becomes – are you planning and living your life in alignment with your best empowerment?

If not, you are either not living your life intentionally, or you are primarily focused upon pleasing other people. I have already written about the need for balance through all aspects of your life, and here is just another example. As you have made choices to connect and interact with other people – for both your human and spiritual purposes – you must still be accountable for your own holistic wellness, growth, and success. Therefore, this idea a setting appropriate goals involves boundaries; and it also clearly encompasses both your personal and professional life.

A large significance to my offering the wisdom that I did in Part I was to encourage you to identify with your higher Authentic Self. And to take steps to assess and discover your unique inner traits and interests as it may lead to pursuing your best work. This authorizes and supports you in intentionally creating the life that is most meaningful and fulfilling to you. And, this directly relates to time management and the goals and expectations you set for yourself – moment-to-moment, day-to-day, etc.

Where possible, boundaries are healthy and necessary. You may certainly encounter relationships and circumstances that demand and require your involvement and priority to some extent – such as bosses, children, partners, etc. Yet this is not a license to abdicate your responsibility for creating your own space and wellness! It is up to you to intentionally choose how and when to honor you. Since virtually everyone around you has their own agenda, do not wait for (or expect) others to care for you in this way.

As for your work, all jobs are different in some way. So in determining the goals and expectations most appropriate for you, you must intentionally and authentically connect to the tasks related to your work. You may have job requirements with a faster or slower pace, human interaction versus computer or "paperwork," project or sales oriented tasks, higher or lower pressure to perform, stronger physical or mental challenges, or many other variables.

Your highest goals and expectations are: to successfully complete your daily tasks according to the expectations of management/ownership. Based upon your true makeup, are these goals and expectations in alignment with your holistic wellness and best career fulfillment? You can either face this question proactively now, or later after things become dissatisfying or perilous.

If you are bringing your greatest mindfulness and best energy to your work and you are still falling behind and stressed, unsatisfied, or unfulfilled, then this is the guidance most meaningful to you. First, you must determine if this is merely temporary, due to specific and unusual circumstance. If not, you must evaluate your schedule-goals to decide if an adjustment or change is warranted.

Career Fulfillment

What is the definition of insanity? Doing the same thing you have always done and expecting a different result. If your goals do not fit your highest wellness and fulfillment, then try something different. But make sure that this is in alignment with your deeper values and truth.

If for whatever reason you are unwilling or unable to shift to a higher state of satisfaction and fulfillment, do your best to incorporate more peace, joy, and acceptance into your current circumstance. In this way you may eventually create the positive energy to shift, or at least be less of a burden upon others.

Another factor in managing your goals and expectations involve an honest assessment of your current energetic state. Only you can decide when you have reached the point of diminishing returns regarding your effort to perform or complete a task. Within yourself, decipher if what you are feeling is fatigue or stress. You may need a break in order to rest your body and refocus your mind.

While performing at your best, you may need to better self-regulate, or otherwise communicate your truth to others who may have unreasonable expectations of you. It takes awareness, courage, and self-love in order to both meet your needs/requirements and promote wellness and success. The key is to live your life and express your truth from the place of your highest identity, values, and integrity. When others notice that your intentions are to do and contribute your best, you will be far less often questioned or doubted.

Honoring the reasonableness and effectiveness of your goals and efforts in any given present moment, is a reflection of higher wisdom and inner strength. Whenever possible, utilize your self-awareness to design your schedule to align with your truth. This will help you to stay balanced and on-track. In the times when extra exertion is required, put your best energy into this "temporary" situation. And then be accountable for scheduling extra recovery time as well.

Honoring Your Commitments

After expressing the importance of boundaries and intentionally honoring your deeper truth, I am going to add another layer. Sometimes we can be so delusional and "reckless" in creating our own schedule that we not only dishonor our own wellness, but we fail to honor our commitments to other people. Even when we have the best of intentions, this is unsatisfactory to us and others.

Therefore, in addition to fulfilling your own needs, you must be able to expand your awareness beyond yourself. And this is a reflection of your emotional intelligence. This will typically require an awakening and reconnection to your higher truth. With a more enlightened perspective you broaden your view to include Unity.

The term "delusion" is a most accurate representation of us when stuck in our ego nature. This is the belief that everything is about us, and that other people should acquiesce on our behalf. It says or implies that, "My needs are more important that yours."

This is not always an intentional act designed to harm another. Most often we are simply stuck in our own fearful energy (in whichever ways this may manifest), and we lack the awareness to notice how this impacts other people. We need a more mindful, selfless approach.

In the management of your time, when you make a commitment to another person you must plan accordingly. If you over commit yourself (for whatever reason), this is your fault not theirs, whether or not it was within your control. The first step is in taking responsibility.

Whether it is an agreement to meet someone at a specific time and place, or for the timely completion of some task, you must strive to honor this commitment. And, if something completely unforeseen prevents you from living up to the agreement, honor yourself and others by communicating this information as quickly, honestly, and empathetically as possible.

Within your greatest state of inner wellness you will value your true self over your ego self, and express your energy accordingly. As you are able to do this, you will naturally recognize and honor other people. You can even use this as a way of prioritizing or setting the proper value to the tasks you schedule. Determine what is most important to do, and what may be eliminated in order to meet your commitments.

Even if this seems like a small thing, it is actually quite significant toward achieving and maintaining career success. How you relate to other people and honor your commitments is a form of expressing energy that directly impacts the quality of the relationship between you and others (co-workers, bosses, etc.). The quality of your connection with other people is a meaningful part of your path to career fulfillment. Don't be so focused upon the quantity of your goals at the expense of the quality of your fulfillment.

Therefore, when you honor your commitments with others you are expressing love on the level of energy. And on the level of human experience you are helping them to meet their own goals and expectations. You will gain trust, appreciation, and create "Good Will." Yet, remain vigilant, and make this a priority, for this gain is easily lost with some people. Always strive to promote true value at work, as this creates success that is mutually beneficial.

CHAPTER 14
Transcending Work Relationships

"When dealing with people, remember that you are not dealing with creatures of logic, but creatures of emotion."

- Dale Carnegie

My previous book in this series is called, *Transcending Relationships: On the Enlightened Path*. Transcending means: Going above and beyond the limits of the usual or ordinary. So, this relates to growing and expanding your energy and perceptions in order to create higher quality relationships of all kinds. In this book on Career Fulfillment, I want to touch upon this concept within your work associations.

The three Parts in Transcending Relationships are: I) Realizing a Higher Truth; II) Learning and Healing from the Past; and III) Offer Your Loving Presence to Others. In this Chapter I will briefly address each of these three concepts relating to your various career relationships, i.e. co-workers, bosses, subordinates, customers, vendors, and other affiliated parties.

Realizing a Higher Truth

There is a higher perspective and truth about all of your human endeavors, and this is equally true concerning your relationships. Beyond how you may have previously defined your relationships, they are actually energy exchange opportunities designed to offer the potential for healing, growth, ascension, and service. Therefore, they serve a higher spiritual purpose.

On a human level, you create many associations that impact your material conditions in either a positive or negative way – as you perceive it. You utilize these connections to coordinate and cooperate with others in an effort to meet your physical needs and desires. Yet, how you go about this is extremely meaningful to your wellness and fulfillment.

Like all other aspects of your existence, where Spirit offers an opportunity to ascend, ego tends to create challenges. The higher path for your relationships is based in the energy of love, which fosters – peace, joy, prosperity, wellness, compassion, service, equality, Unity, etc. On the other side, ego is based in the energy of fear, which often demotes you to – division, anger, greed, anxiety, judgment, lack, selfishness, discrimination, etc.

As always, since we exist and reside in both identities (while human), our lives become about integrating and balancing our higher qualities into our human experience. The more we develop the tools of self-mastery, the more we may intentionally express our loving energy. In any case, it is an on-going moment-to-moment process. Even when it does not appear so, within our relationships we have an opportunity to support our healing, growth, and ascension.

It is your relationships that reflect back to you your inner level of wellness and need for healing. When viewing this from a more enlightened perspective, this is designed to serve as a tool in your growth and evolution. Through the quality of the energy exchanged, you have an opportunity to shift and realign to a more loving and empowering connection.

Within a more traditional view, you may look upon a particular human connection as supportive-unsupportive, joyful-painful, comfortable-uncomfortable, etc. This relates largely to your perspective of yourself – your inner energetic state – and the lessons you have yet to learn. Therefore, your best strategy for creating transcending relationships is to view them from a more enlightened perspective – which utilizes wisdom, mindfulness, and personal accountability.

Focus and develop your awareness to recognize how YOU are impacting (for better or worse) your own inner wellness and happiness as a result of your relationships and interactions. You have the power of creation regarding the quality of your experience. Therefore, facilitate your own healing and growth; and stop expecting other people to simply change their behavior for your benefit.

Within a position of higher consciousness, you have the power to shift your perception of others, and consider them as teachers rather than offenders. In truth, their mission is not to upset or harm you. Typically, they are merely living within their own ego-delusion (when not offering their loving presence). And, when you feel personally challenged by this, you must look within yourself for the answers to your healing, growth, and transcendence.

Be accountable for offering yourself the love and light that you are expecting others to provide. Then, within this level of empowerment, be more mindful of accepting other people as they are, and not as you wish them to be. They are doing their best within the conditions they have created for themselves, so always offer your kindness and compassion.

You are responsible for your energetic expressions; your outer display in terms of thoughts, words, feelings, and actions to be received by others. On some level they will feel and respond to this energy, even if you are unaware of this connection. While you are not responsible for their interpretations and delusions, always endeavor to apply your best integrity within your work relations.

You may have heard the concept that we, on some level, mirror each other. For example, if I am feeling an abundance of inner fear or self-doubt within a particular situation or circumstance, I am more likely to attract someone to reflect this inner belief back to me through their words or actions. This may feel quite challenging to me, and consequently, I may feel angry or hurt by this person. In truth, I am playing a role in this drama.

Conversely, when I am feeling more confident and self-assured, I am more likely to encounter those who treat me in a supportive and positive way. My inner energy is in a state of wellness, love, and empowerment. Therefore, I am expressing this on the level of energy, which elevates the quality of my thoughts, words, and actions. This should illustrate how your inner wellness and self-love are so critical to your success and fulfillment.

Additionally, you can learn about your own energy and wellness by assessing the primary energetic quality of those with whom you choose to spend your time. As you elevate your energy and consciousness, you will be less inclined to remain connected with those who are both consumed by negativity AND unwilling to be accountable for their own growth. On your path to enlightenment you are becoming incompatible.

Internally, you are typically balancing conflicting beliefs – self-love and self-judgment – to various degrees. Therefore, you naturally attract people who will present these positive or negative qualities back to you. However, the point is not to identify with this feedback, but instead to realize this as confirmation of the predominant state of your own energy.

From your place of personal accountability you may then take the steps to shift your energy and otherwise support your own healing. Your goal is always to be connected to your own loving energy. And this directly supports your wellness and that of the others connected to you.

As opposed to avoiding experiences or interactions, you must endeavor to maintain your best inner strength in any circumstance. This, of course, is more challenging during times when you are controlled by ego. Which is why your focus upon the present moment, and connection to your Authentic Self, is so valuable to your humanity. Your best power resides within a connection to your own inner loving energy.

Otherwise, when other people express their ego-based energy to you, your first reaction might be to feel wounded and then either lash out at them or otherwise feel defeated and deflated within. Instead of fighting ego with ego, learn to just pause for a moment and breathe. Use this time to intentionally re-connect to and identify with your self-love – your truth. Remember that you are responsible for your own wellness, and what other people do, say, or think about you does not define you. They are representing their own self-beliefs, understandings, delusions, and level of consciousness, which in some way was triggered within their connection to you.

Therefore, continue to reinforce the energy of love within you in order to maintain your strength. When you are best able to do so, evaluate the situation to see if you contributed on the level of energy. If you recognize that you made an unloving expression, again, apply your best integrity to help rectify the situation. And then turn your focus upon any issues of self-healing (usually shifting to greater self-love and higher truth) that are needed to support your own inner state of wellness at this time.

This is how you are being accountable to yourself and others. As you become more adept at being responsible for yourself you will more naturally notice the goodness in others. Now you will more easily create transcending relationships.

I am not telling you that this is always easy. For if it was, humanity would look very differently. However, I am saying that this is a process of shifting the energy within yourself, and between you and others. And a whole different set of circumstances and opportunities may now present themselves that will encourage a positive outcome for all involved.

So, look upon your relationship interactions as a way to recognize the energy being expressed by you, for the purposes of further healing and growth. And also develop the awareness and inner strength to maintain and express your truth to others in a loving and supportive way. Your work relationships, even the more difficult ones, are there to guide and teach you to honor your deeper truth, and to further develop your opportunities for growth and service.

Learning and Healing from the Past

Depending upon your age and exposure to the working world, you likely have had many past relationship experiences. These were situations and circumstances in which you expressed and received energy with and amongst other people as part of your job. The quality of this exchange was based upon your level of inner wellness and consciousness at the time, though you may have simply judged other people as helpful and kind, or distasteful and abusive.

In truth, this represented your ability to connect with others from either the energy of self-love or fear, and from a higher understanding of the identity and value of all people. As is always true, it was less about them and more about you. So, for whatever you experienced, with a higher wisdom you now have an opportunity to transcend the past – to heal, grow, and evolve.

Especially early in our career, we are relatively emotionally immature and insecure. This will attract many experiences within our work relationships where our ego-delusion will feel threatened and defeated. Not having developed the tools and EQ to handle this in a loving and empowered way, we are likely to store up some debilitating negative energy that impacts us for many years.

Regarding any false and disempowering past energy that still resides within, you have two healthy choices. One, if possible for you, choose to utilize your wisdom to simply release this energy that is unsupportive and no longer valid today. And then, replace it with your loving truth in the present.

Or two, for experiences that are more overpowering, assess the specific experience and follow the process of energetic healing from Chapter 7. Develop the higher awareness of your power, and connection to your truth. In any case, your past experiences only hold the power over you in the present that you yourself allow.

We have typically created a balance of satisfying, encouraging, and enjoyable experiences, to go along with the ones that felt unsatisfying, discouraging, and unpleasant. While we desire to repeat and create only the favorable experiences, they all serve a valuable and necessary purpose. Often times it is the seemingly negative experiences that have the most to teach us, and therefore, are critical to our development.

This is because they did not just "happen to us," they were created by us. So, you must begin to shift to a higher awareness and understanding of that which you created for your own higher purposes. This willingness to be accountable for enlightened growth is the process of your evolution – leading to greater fulfillment.

I know that this may be contrary your previous education, and not always easy to accept. I also want to clarify that you are not responsible for the hurtful or harmful actions of other people. However, on some level or degree you participated in the interaction, experience, or event. And your goal for healing and growth is to understand your part in the experience in order to shift to a higher energy that supports you in creating and attracting more positive outcomes in the future.

Sometimes your experience is the culminating consequence of errant and unwise choices you have previously made. And this represents a lesson for greater wisdom and accountability. So, endeavor to understand this without ego judgment of yourself, and utilize this information toward being wiser in the present.

In other times your past experiences are simply a part of your process for learning and understanding your true value, potential, and preferences. Regarding your career, you must learn many things through the process of life experience. "What type of person or company is most supportive, or unsupportive, to my success and well-being?" Therefore, the lesson has value now, regardless of what we may have thought of the experience at the time.

When you do not take such an enlightened approach, your ego-nature may wreak havoc on your perceptions and energy. You are disappointed that something did not work out the way you desired. And for whatever reason, you were heavily invested in a particular outcome. So, you remove yourself from accountability by blaming others for your suffering. And concurrently, you hold the negative fearful energies of guilt, shame, sadness, and failure.

As common as this may be, it is a position of weakness that confirms your fear and powerlessness. And to a degree you continue to allow this poison to affect certain relationships and experiences today. On some level it actually was your inner belief in fear that attracted this past situation, circumstance, or lesson. And even while you claim your innocence and blame the others involved, deep within you know that in some way you betrayed or dishonored yourself.

This is where we may recognize our need to heal and grow. Therefore, we must be accountable for all that we have created in order to take full responsibility for our own wellness (an internal process) that leads to wisdom and growth. This requires our self-forgiveness, which is the first step to releasing this disempowering energy within. And then, through an enlightened perspective, we may release enough ego to forgive all others involved.

Within the context of past work experiences, you may have had a difficult time associating or connecting with certain co-workers, bosses, subordinates, customers, etc. In truth, they were not there to burden you. They were simply functioning within their own delusion. Yet, even if you felt harmed in some fashion, you now may realize the true purpose of the connection. This is your opportunity for development and fulfillment, once you are able to accept the experience from your higher place of self-awareness, true identity, and wisdom.

With your full intention and loving power you may view the circumstances of your life in a manner that is most supportive for you in the present. Do not get hung up in your judgement about "them," or the arbitrary "right or wrong." Through wisdom you need to know that you are not capable, responsible, or authorized to change or "fix" others. You are only empowered to facilitate your own growth opportunities.

So, endeavor to go to your sacred inner reflective space to connect with your truth. Release your ego as best you can, and observe this situation more objectively. You are not determining "right or wrong" in the abstract, because everyone will judge this differently according to their own perspective. You are looking for the ways in which you may more fully honor your deeper truth – which is always seeking to reside in self-love and Unity.

It will be helpful to seek the answers to the following questions: How may I shift and elevate my energy in connection with this other person? How may I elevate my energy to simply accept them as they are, without feeling depleted myself? What is the role of this person within the process of my own highest development? How may I transcend my own fearful energy to the extent that I may only express kindness and support to them? Are they still supportive to me ongoing, or have they fulfilled their role, and is it now my best option to disconnect from this person?

As you are able to connect to this wisdom, you become more secure within your inner power. You are not basing your feelings or self-beliefs upon the actions or judgments of others. You are seeking the higher ground from which to offer your best service and integrity. Additionally, you are now serving others by showing them a more loving way to function. This is the enlightened path.

Offer Your Loving Presence

Having shifted and elevated your inner energy and beliefs, you are now more empowered to offer your loving presence to all. Even if this term does not sound like it applies to work or business, it is always your higher truth. Therefore, it is the best and most supportive space from which to create career fulfillment and success.

As you develop and learn to function within this space more often, you are creating greater value and contribution at work. This is because you are now working within expansive (rather than restrictive) energy. Certainly, as your energy ebbs and flows, you may experience a variety of conditions at work that may impact the quality of your energy exchanges. Plus, you will encounter others who are residing within their own level of consciousness, wellness, and perspective that differs from yours.

Therefore, the greater your ability to remain connected to your loving presence, the more you are able to experience and integrate higher values within all of these variables and qualities at work. Therefore, focus on maintaining your inner strength, self-love, mindfulness, and acceptance of others. This

Career Fulfillment

is your ongoing practice for personal growth and holistic wellness that supports career fulfillment.

On the enlightened path your sea may be less turbulent, and your love for yourself and others more unwavering. This of course is more conducive to the fulfillment of your professional goals, as well as, cooperation and teamwork, impeccable communication, and your best contribution to others.

Your loving presence is primarily a function and representation of your inner state and higher identity, and this then manifests as your outer expression to all of those with whom you interact. Know that you are always being recognized, judged, and valued based upon other people's perceptions of your energy. This is not only true for your words and actions, but even your demeanor, and the more subtle energetic expressions. You are always communicating your inner truth, so be accountable for healing and elevating your energy.

Offering your loving presence reveals a sense of inner wellness that is supportive and comforting to others. When contributing toward your job with this higher energy, you are more naturally encouraging the finest in those around you. You are authentically offering your best, with only the highest intentions for the success of all.

Whether or not others can raise their game to this level need not be impactful regarding your commitment for loving service. You are now primarily focused upon your inner motivation and empowerment. Being accountable for all you create, you now define your best criteria for success. .

Your goal is the fulfillment and satisfaction of doing your best in all situations. Plus, it turns out that this is the most effective way to be recognized as a valuable team member. And, this is most supportive toward receiving the acclaim and material rewards we all desire. This is the integration of your spirituality into your humanity in the attainment of your highest career fulfillment.

CHAPTER 15
Cooperation and Unity

"Thousands of candles can be lit from a single candle, and the life of the candle will not be shortened. Happiness never decreases by being shared."

- Buddha

Moving Toward Enlightenment

Career fulfillment requires alignment with your higher truth, which supports inner-strength and wellness, leading to deeper meaning and purpose. These are inner developments that become the outer expressions of your higher value and contribution. Yet, your success is also interdependent to your connections with other people. You each play a role in either assisting or suppressing your mutual success at work.

Individually and collectively your growth and ascension necessitates that you work in unison with many others. Within this endeavor I am offering Cooperation and Unity as enlightened principles; the goal of which is mutual success.

Unfortunately, in our ego-driven definition of success, the term cooperation has come to be defined as somewhat passive or weak. We are told to be the leader, the top dog, the alpha – to standout above the rest. Therefore, within this mindset, I may feel that supporting you is not in my best interest. Therefore, what is my motivation to "cooperate" in your success?

In truth, this attitude is weakness and delusion. Cooperation with the intention of giving and receiving your best is a sign of great inner-strength and self-love. This is the purpose and natural expansion of a higher definition of success.

When endeavoring to live (and work) enlightened we will consider more than our immediate gratification and self-interest. We take the more encompassing longer term view of sustainable fulfillment, wellness, and abundance. The healthiest path is always more important than the outcome, because it exists in the power of each present moment.

Clearly, the old view of career success has focused on short-term "wins" that lead us to pursue our own wealth and power; and often without regard to its cost to others (or the Earth). In this context, any warped view of cooperation would be as a temporary strategy toward personal gain. Therefore, if you still believe whole-heartedly that this is the best model for success, you must also accept that the great suffering that this causes is suitable as well.

Hopefully, since you are reading a book called *Career Fulfillment*, you are looking to improve the energy in the world, and promote greater cooperation and Unity. In which case, you may opt to become more accountable for choosing to fulfill a path of success that does not, by its very nature, harm others. And it is my job to help you understand how this is possible.

Often, when we feel disempowered, we are quick to judge other people as being corrupt; as willing to abuse, manipulate, and denigrate for some personal gain. See world history and current events for plenty of examples. Yet, even while we criticize this behavior, on a deeper level, we have accepted that this is THE path to get what we want.

We believe that the oppressors are "winners" because they found a way to acquire wealth and/or position.

Consequently, we have tolerated and even secretly admired them. Yet, we have been blinded by our delusion, which misses the truth about the true quality of their lives. When we function within the lower energy of fear, we are unable to sufficiently express and receive the true energy of integrity, respect, and love. This is intrinsically unfulfilling and unsatisfying, regardless of our life style or affluence.

Therefore, we ourselves must ascend to a position, whereby, our highest intention at work is to lead with integrity – for the good of all. Without this shift, we will be hard pressed to sustain career fulfillment, or embark on any kind of evolutionary path. This is a personal awakening that then supports us toward expressing more loving qualities in our career.

Release your "admiration" for those who lack integrity and behave in unscrupulous ways. But don't waste your energy hating or despising them either. Literally begin to shift your focus away from this model or specific individuals. If role models are important to your process of development, seek those who serve with kindness, compassion, and loving energy. Love the light rather than hate the darkness.

Your work goals of achieving happiness, abundance, and fulfillment will come from functioning within the energetic qualities that align with these results. These are supported through integrity, cooperation, and Unity. Your personal growth work is to elevate your perception of yourself as a whole, empowered, loving person. As you are more successful in this, you will more readily accept others in this higher view as well. And your natural inclination will be to work together to support each other on a higher path.

Through enlightenment we intentionally focus our energy toward the light, and allow the darkness to extinguish itself.

We know that cooperation is working together in the pursuit of mutually beneficial goals. Unity is a term that expresses the very nature of all beings as united, and of a common origin and identity. This implies that we are all equal, valuable, worthy, and empowered. As Prince sang in *Let's Go Crazy*, "Dearly beloved, we are gathered here together to get through this thing called life." It is for each of us to live and function within this higher principle, or otherwise to continue on our current path of limitation, dissatisfaction, and destruction.

Some will find all of this a bit "heavy," in a teaching about work and career fulfillment. Yet, any teaching from a holistic perspective should consider the deeper meaning and consequences that impact our overall wellness. We spend so much of our energy and focus upon our jobs (including income, status, contribution, and service); so, this is a good place to shift to a higher perspective, for greater gain.

It's time to transcend the old business model and attitudes around work. This starts through the inner healing, growth, and ascension of enough people who have a higher vision for themselves and humanity. We have newer generations that may decide that it is important to define their success in ways that also contribute to the value and well-being of others.

And, hopefully, there will be many from older generations that will awaken to accept their responsibility to improve the world that they will leave behind. This can be in big or small ways depending upon your unique path, career opportunities and choices. Within this new culture, if you are unwilling to support your co-workers and associates, or promote the qualities of cooperation and Unity, you cannot rightfully consider yourself as successful.

In order for employers to flourish in a more conscious way, this is the energy that must be encouraged and supported throughout their businesses and organizations. Consciousness is a higher model for humanity, and it must become more prevalent within our daily lives. And since the way in which we typically spend the greatest amount of time and energy is in our career, this is most applicable at work.

An elevation of consciousness raises our vibration to recognize our truth as "spiritual beings having a human experience." And, as spiritual beings we have a higher calling. The human experience, in this case, is our working together to accomplish personal fulfillment and evolution for all.

Ascension to this truth and identity is required in order to promote Unity, equality, and the higher value of all people; regardless of their specific job title. And this will aid and encourage more people to become employed and to contribute. Cooperation and Unity consciousness become a moment-to-moment motivation and intention for expressing this form of love to all involved in connection to our jobs.

Practical Application

On a daily basis you are attempting to satisfactorily complete the numerous tasks of your job, according to the requirements and expectations established within the organization. This is your **minimal** goal and focus. If you do not fulfill this you may likely lose your job and income. So, even as a lower level of intention, performing your work at a basic level is certainly important. However, is this enough for success and deeper fulfillment?

As you are learning a new job, or meeting significant demands, this may be all that you can manage. All of your faculties are primarily motivated toward simply keeping up. Yet, going forward, as you are applying your best wisdom, mindfulness, and accountability, you are empowered to do more.

Accordingly, you endeavor to take every opportunity to bring and express your best energy within the function of your job. And therefore, "how" you do your job, and "how" this impacts others, is vitally important to your success. Your intention is to extend far beyond the minimal requirements for just keeping your employment.

The simplest way of effectively doing this is to engage in a more supportive and accommodating energy with your co-workers. As you do this, you are more self-assured and free to speak and act in positive, thoughtful, and encouraging ways. In addition to doing your job to the best of your ability, this initially begins with your attitudes and perceptions.

As you shift your energy to align with your greater loving presence, you will naturally feel more secure and worthy of your own fulfillment. And now you become more comfortable living your truth at work. This allows you to shift your energetic expressions from fear and self-protection to love and cooperation.

Cooperation becomes sharing. Knowing that you are accountable for your own wellness, you no longer need to take advantage of anyone else. You are giving and contributing your best for its own sake. So, you easily share the workload (where possible), the credit for success, and the responsibility for improvement.

We always share (through our expressions) the energy that is most prevalent from within. When we develop our inner-strength and self-love, our thoughts, words, and actions naturally offer the higher qualities of love to all. Our focus is more on giving to others, and honoring ourselves.

So instead of basing your outer support on how another person relates to you, learn to offer your best inner qualities to all. Otherwise, you will only cooperate with those certain individuals you "like" or agree with, but not those who disturb (annoy, bother, anger, etc.) you. Again, we are taking responsibility for our own inner wellness, as we express the best energy for the benefit of all.

It costs you nothing to come to work with a smile instead of a dark demeanor. It is all about honoring yourself and respecting others. If you simply cannot stand the job you have, there are only two choices in order to limit your suffering, and that of your co-workers. One, you can get a different (hopefully better) job. Or two, if that is not presently possible, you must shift your energy and attitude to express more light. Think more often about what you can contribute, rather than what you feel you need from others.

For whatever job you *choose* to do, find value and purpose in doing your job well, and begin to support others with more positive energy. In truth, when you start to look beyond your own needs and desires in order to support another, it intrinsically lifts your spirit and energy. Your perceptions go a very long way toward creating your reality. If you only look at what you have as bleak or lacking, than that is what you will continue to experience.

Cooperation and Unity is energy that becomes tangible on a material level as it manifests into your experiences and relationships. Cooperation is synonymous with teamwork. So, in addition to shifting and elevating your energy, offer your assistance and encouragement whenever possible. You are each team members of your company, and accordingly, you have a common goal of contributing to the success of the whole.

In order to sustain your ability to offer this level of cooperation and support to all "team members," you must elevate your identity and your view of theirs. I have already spent much time in Part I explaining that your true identity is your Authentic or Spiritual Self. And this pertains as much to your work personae as in any other aspect of your human experience.

Functioning from this place will best support you in accepting all others as having a Divine identity as well. Some people may know or sense this for themselves, and more often act in a positive way. Others will function completely unaware of their true identity and loving power. They may be lost in the darkness of their ego-delusion, as we all are from time-to-time. This is not for you to judge, within the principles of cooperation and Unity, it is only for you to accept the higher potential in all people.

From this perspective you may more easily return only kindness and support to those who act out in "ugly" and fearful ways. You may choose to continue to reside in your peace, strength, and love anyway. This is the enlightened path, and it encourages the expression of loving energy leading to the greatest opportunities for success and fulfillment for all.

As you share your best energy through cooperation you will connect on that level with more people. Again, even if an equal quality of energy is not initially reciprocated, continue to align with your higher truth internally and express your loving energy as your authentic purpose. This is a building block or tool for your career success, and a higher example to others.

Learn to avoid "attaching" to the negativity of co-workers and others. Do them and yourself a favor by not participating in their complaints and dissatisfaction. I have seen a great deal of productive time wasted in commiseration with other employees. You are not their therapist, so don't encourage them down their dark path (or feed their fear). Be the example of light and loving energy that is focused on joy, satisfaction, and production. This will do more to lift their energy than affirming their victim mentality.

The greatest hindrance to individual and mutual success at work comes from two places. First, as I have discussed in some detail, a lack of energetic wellness (overwhelming fear) within us as individuals. This directly promotes selfishness, protectiveness, and isolation. It says, "I am going to get mine, regardless of how that impacts the welfare of others." This is not cooperation or Unity – it is fear, which breeds suffering.

The second hindrance comes from the culture, structure, goals, values, and awareness of management and ownership. The energy expressed at the head of the company will directly and indirectly impact the consciousness of its workers and associates. If they are focused upon their own enrichment and importance over the well-being and success of the employees, then their energy will have a detrimental impact upon the workers and company. Therefore, it is imperative that as entrepreneurs and managers we develop and maintain the ideals of love and Unity within a more conscious business model, as the higher standard of success.

CHAPTER 16
Impeccable Communication

"Think twice before you speak, because your words and influence will plant the seed of either success or failure in the mind of another."

- Napoleon Hill

Most everyone knows that communication is a key to any successful endeavor in which you are relying upon and working with other people. And as always, your most enlightened external expressions will be initiated from your healthiest internal energetic state. Certainly there are skills to be learned that enhance communication at work. Yet, your awareness and intention for delivering and receiving words with impeccability are essential.

There are two primary aspects to effective communication, and naturally they involve the two parts of communication – speaking and listening. The first involves how and what we express as our message to the listener. And the second pertains to our ability to honor others, as we receive and interpret their words and message.

Impeccable Speaking

With mindfulness, consider your inner energetic state and true purpose for communicating with a specific person at the time you choose to do so. This impacts the "how" you are communicating. Regarding this, here are some questions to consider.

Are you speaking from a thoughtful and loving space? Or, are you venting or threatening from your place of inner fear or anger? And, are your intentions to uplift your audience or peacefully resolve any issues in a mutually supportive way. Or, are you speaking in ways that are designed to bully, manipulate, or undermine others (expressions based in fear)?

It seems rather obvious as to how the impact of these energies (and words) may be received by other people. And yet, how often do you express yourself in a harsh, inconsiderate, or negative way, and still expect something positive to come from it? Is your purpose to accomplish something constructive or simply to be heard? Always endeavor to connect with your best presence and awareness before you speak.

Next, you must consider "what" you are expressing. Does it reflect your truth; is it "small-talk;" or is it simply some objective information? This will determine the degree to which you are attached to your message energetically. And in turn, this defines the amount of inner expectation you may have toward a certain response or reply from your audience.

When simply communicating objective data, which occurs often at work, you are not personally identified with this information. It may be right or wrong, good or bad, but it is not a reflection of your personal value or identity. Therefore, you relate to others as the messenger and not the message. Your ego is not attached to this information or any particular reply.

Regarding small-talk, this is usually casual banter. It generally is a message that is unattached to your deeper identity. You may have some ulterior motive or agenda attached to the conversation. In any case, your dependency upon a certain response or validation is generally minimal.

However, when you are sharing your deeper perceptions or beliefs (whether truth or ego-delusion), you may associate this information with a part of your value or identity. Consequently, you feel an amount of vulnerability. Therefore, your ego may have a strong preference that this message be received with support and agreement. Based on this, you will either feel validated or offended by the response of your audience. And this will likely affect the tenor and direction of future communications.

From a more enlightened perspective, this is where you must learn to accept that your truth does not always coincide with that of other people. Therefore, your connection to self-love and inner strength must be stronger. This will assist you in maintaining your inner peace and love, regardless of outside influences. Even while your attachment to approval may be strong, with awareness you can simply choose to honor yourself while allowing others to live in their truth. This will take great intention and practice, and necessitates an amount of healing and growth.

However, when your attachment to ego gets the best of you, your natural inclination is to defend your position (beliefs and perspective). How you are then able to manage your inner energetic state will often dictate the effectiveness of future communications with this person, and perhaps the quality of the relationship going forward.

If you sink into ego-nature, you position yourself for battle. And you may likely create further hurt feelings from which to overcome. Depending upon the situation, real damage may be done.

Therefore, your enlightened intention must be: "This is my meaning and feeling on the subject, you are certainly entitled to have a different opinion." From here, depending upon the issue to be resolved or mediated, you may either reside in your truth or choose to make some concession. You are still supporting the principles of cooperation and Unity, and therefore, you have a willingness to open your mind and heart with acceptance of other views. And, as always, you are utilizing your highest emotional intelligence in this process.

This is why mindfulness and connection to your Authentic Self is so valuable in everyday living. Your level of consciousness greatly impacts your communications and interactions for better or worse. Again, if you are simply relaying objective data to someone else, this typically will not attach to your self-belief, and therefore, not engage your ego. It simply becomes a matter of accuracy – and not a judgment of your value.

Here are some appropriate questions regarding your intention or purpose for communicating. Why are you offering this message to this person at this time? Is this primarily for your benefit or theirs? Are you simply venting, or are you asking for their assistance or feedback? Are you delivering a message that is generally supportive, or gossip and negativity that is energetically destructive? Are you intending to express an opinion or state a fact? Do you really have something of value to say, or do you just want to hear yourself talk? Is now the most appropriate time to engage in this communication, or should it be delayed or simply remain a thought in your head?

This first step to communicating clearly is to be clear about the purpose and intent of your message. Likely, we have all witnessed or engaged in each of the variables listed above. And accordingly, we may acknowledge some communications to be either successful or unsuccessful. However, impeccable communication rises to a higher standard. On the enlightened path you will be more intentional in creating communications that offer and enhance light and love.

If you really want to be heard for YOUR benefit, let your audience know this. Tell them in advance: "I just need to vent for a moment, do you mind hearing me out." And then thank them for their support. You won't want to do this too often at work, or to just anyone. Yet, certain people will give you this courtesy, and it can be supportive to your well-being. And then, at times you will be required to reciprocate this support for their benefit.

Notice your speaking habits. Talking over someone or dominating the conversation is inconsiderate to the listener. This is decidedly not impeccable. Your ego is displaying an overwhelming need to be heard and validated. This is a sign that your focus is upon getting your needs met to the exclusion of others.

In this case, you are likely dealing with insecurity that is in need of healing. Transcendence of this habit requires greater mindfulness and self-love. Know that you are valuable and worthy all on your own, without constantly needing to show off or convince others. As you are able to love yourself more, you will be able to open up the space for valuing and honoring others through the act of listening.

As often as possible, find your purpose in expressing your words for the benefit of others. Are they in need of information or inspiration? Are they asking for your opinion or input? There is a healthy balance of knowing when to talk and when to keep your thoughts to yourself. And the deciding factor may be – "who is benefiting by my expression of this message?" Again, refer to Chapter 8, and the development of emotional intelligence.

If your clear sense is that this in some way supports the listener, then fire away. Otherwise, take a few breaths and consider your true intentions for speaking. Not all of your thoughts need to be expressed to others. At the very least, avoid statements that unnecessarily bring harm to yourself or others.

Another way to support more impeccable speaking is to transcend the habit of using accusatory statements. For example: "You did this to me (or the company)," or "You made me feel this way, when you …." In order to be more effective (and enlightened), take responsibility for your experiences, perceptions, feelings, etc.

If you want to make a positive impact and resolve an issue, don't immediately put others on the defensive. Instead, you may say, "I felt 'this' way when 'this' happened." Now you can have discussion about interpretation and perception, instead of blame. Or, acknowledge the challenging situation that has occurred based upon certain decisions or actions, without condemning anyone. Always deal with the reality of situations from the standpoint of integrity, resolution, and higher energetic expressions.

From the standpoint of speaking, another highly beneficial practice is to show consideration and interest in other people. Through your words you have the ability to draw in other people by allowing them to talk about themselves or otherwise express their truth. So, ask questions that show you care. Otherwise, when you constantly make the conversation for and about you they will naturally lose interest.

With your focus on impeccable speaking you will always seek the highest ground, and results that are mutually beneficial. At work this is a critical part of success. Differences of opinion or desired outcome may be resolved peaceful without a message of retribution, or the buildup of harmful thoughts. As you first honor your higher Self, you will more easily honor all others within the principles of cooperation and Unity. This leads to personal fulfillment and the success of the team.

Impeccable Listening

The next aspect of impeccable communication is in the listening, the other side of the coin. Again, awareness is your greatest tool. And, you are required to utilize your best energetic presence and emotional intelligence.

You can safely assume that other people want to be heard and they want to talk about themselves. You honor them when you listen attentively. As best you can, let them finish their thought or message without jumping to conclusions or planning your reply. If their monologue runs on-and-on, you are not obligated to forfeit your time needlessly. After a "reasonable" period, simply interject in a polite way. You can either inform them that you have something to say, or that you need to move on to another activity (conversation, etc.).

When you are not in a position (for whatever reason) to have the type of meaningful conversation that a situation requires, you can express this truth as considerately as possible. Then, suggest an alternative approach or time. Always be accountable for your wellness, but do so with loving intention.

We utilize our utmost focus by limiting the chatter and obsessive self-interest in our own mind. This requires us to be present and to maintain our own inner wellness and peace. The consideration we show others by fully listening will encourage them to express their truth and to care about ours. This is the give and take that makes your communication most effective and productive.

If you are speaking face-to-face, you may offer direct eye contact, and otherwise express your body language as receptive. If the speaker is aligned with their awareness, they will likely know when you are present or not. So do your best to honor others with your listening.

It is more than simply a matter of manners; you want to gain and contribute the greatest value for all involved within the time you allocate for your communications. While it is important to have some light conversation and banter, it is good to keep in mind the value of time management. This is especially true at work. There is no benefit in wasting anyone's time, either unwilling or unable to engage in impeccable communication.

We typically find it more common to show proper respect (listening skills) to those with some form of authority over us. This is another example of ego control, wanting someone's approval and seeking our own self-interest. It's not that this is inappropriate. However, I am suggesting that when communicating impeccably we honor ourselves and ALL others – always.

Once you determine that a specific communication is beneficial for all involved, learn to say what you mean – and mean what you say. On the enlightened path there is less game playing and a more sincere exchange of value. As you desire the best for all parties (and not just yourself), truth will flow more easily and effortlessly.

Along these lines, gossip is a no-no. A common practice at work is to complain to co-workers about your job, boss, other co-workers, home life, etc. There are jealousies, misunderstandings, misinformation, and false perceptions that need not be expressed to others – as they offer no value or benefit. Any time you judge others, or they judge you, it is always about the person doing the judging. Focus on healing your own insecurities and fear, and speak the truth with positive intention. I have seen countless examples in my 30 years in business of how damaging this "loose talk" is to the perception and reputation of people.

While communicating impeccably we take responsibility for ourselves. We understand the power of our words, as energy that manifests into the quality of our experiences and relationships. With respect to listening, you need not oblige anyone who is engaging in destructive verbalization. Simply and politely express your unwillingness to gossip or speak negatively about people not present.

This is not only a way to maintain your best energy, but also is an example to others of your integrity. You show yourself to be trustworthy and respectful. If you must vent about your work on occasion, do it with those you trust who are unaffiliated with your employment.

Use the Most Effective Communication Method

The success of any interpersonal relationship, including those at work, requires effective communication. This not only involves speaking and listening impeccably, but also utilizing the most appropriate method of communication to elicit the desired result. What is your goal in deciding to express a particular message with another person? Then, as you answer this question, tailor your methodology to this message.

As they say, things get lost in translation. You express a message that means one thing to you, which is then interpreted by another person in an entirely different way, according to their own point of view. As you probably have experienced, this can sometimes be disastrous. Especially in these times when so many communications are done electronically and not face-to-face.

It is very important to know your audience. You are not assured that other people are always being honest with you, but do the best you can to decipher their traits and intentions. What I have learned is that if there is any doubt about someone misconstruing your message, error on the side of over explaining in a considerate tone. I have seen both professionally and personally where my intentions were pure and well-meaning, yet my message was received negatively. This is especially true for email.

I recommend that sensitive conversations be done in person or over the telephone whenever possible. This allows for voice inflections, which offer further evidence of the meaning and context of your message. It also provides an immediate opportunity to clarify your words.

Texting is a great way to share small amounts of information in a timely way. As for email, consider your audience carefully. While communicating as an accountant it was appropriate for me to give a message without the subtext of emotion. This always worked fine in submissions to other "accounting types." Yet, I learned that those with more of a "marketing or emotional" makeup, at times found my messages to be "short" or "harsh."

Of course, this was not my intent. But it shows you the importance of considering the perspective of your audience, and adjusting accordingly. Now, this "accounting vs marketing" example is a generalization, however, it brings out the point intended. You likely have your own experiences of ineffective communication at work. Endeavor to learn and grow from your past mistakes – enlightenment is a process.

With proper awareness and accountability you will more adequately choose the most appropriate method for communication. Since we are all unique, there are as many varying levels of consciousness as there are speakers and listeners. Therefore, you will not always have perfect communication, no matter how careful or considerate you are. The point is to be present within your higher self and do your best to support and honor all involved. This represents impeccable communication on the enlightened path.

CHAPTER 17
Joy and Satisfaction

"The worst days of those who enjoy what they do, are better than the best days of those who don't."

- E. James Rohn

The Joy is in the Journey

Just so you know, this is not a frivolous intention for your career. In fact, can you really experience true fulfillment without joy and satisfaction? Wait, isn't work supposed to be hard and burdensome? The point of enlightenment is that work (and life) can be what you make of it.

Even in the times when little seems to be going your way, focus your energy toward enjoying the journey and appreciating your efforts. You are attempting to do your best, and eventually this will pay off. In fact, it is very important to cultivate these qualities at work. Not only as a balance to the many challenges, but also as the catalyst for facilitating your growth, evolution, and contribution on a greater level.

The deepest truth is that joy and satisfaction are internal qualities that lead to fulfillment – on both the level of your Soul and humanity. However, our prevalent worldly education has supported self-preservation, which emphasizes that our focus be upon our external qualities, conditions, and interactions. Additionally, when controlled by our fear (ego), joy and satisfaction seem out-of-reach.

This has worked to devalue the power and purpose of your journey. You all too easily become impatient for the prized outcome, or the happiness based on some future event. But this illusion causes you to miss the inner joy available throughout the process of your work and life.

Most of us have learned to depend upon other people, as we define success in a very incomplete way. And based upon this view, we determine our own value by way of comparison to the attributes, achievement, and conditions that other people experience. We don't particularly care about their journey or ups-and-downs, we only covet their rewards.

Can you see that this is not only delusional, but also creates a virtual certainty that you will NOT experience or sustain true joy, satisfaction, and wellness? You must reside in your reality as you honor and express your true potential. Through these on-going intentions and efforts you may realize the moment-to-moment process of your best life.

Until you can define and realize your own wellness and fulfillment within, you will most often feel lack, fear, and even hopelessness. Expecting other people to provide your joy and satisfied is a losing battle. The best path is to align your efforts and intentions to connect with your own unique qualities of higher truth and value. In this you may accept your own path and recognize your process, as it is, with appreciation.

Supporting your Joy and Satisfaction at Work

When you dishonor or abandon your sacred energetic space, you will tend to be overly concerned with what others believe or possess. You cease to remember that in the present you are enough. Your focus may then shift toward anxiety for an unknowable future, or some "victimization" from your past. These perceptions are not based in reality, and are therefore, disempowering.

The truth is that it is your job to awaken and shift your awareness toward a path that aligns with your higher purpose and identity – this is your true reality. You must develop a new language of self-talk, and a new value system that is more accessible and meaningful to you. Only you can define and recognize these qualities of joy and satisfaction within yourself.

More often than not, your deeper fulfillment will occur in small ways and will go unnoticed by others. It comes in the moments of presence in which you are doing your best, honoring your truth, and accomplishing the task before you. It is the process of experiencing your human life, while aligned with Spirit that is most joyful and satisfying.

Learn to look for these feelings in connection to your work. Begin to find your purpose in moments of fulfillment, and then realize this as true success. As you are able to string these experiences together you may notice a higher level of overall competency and contribution. Since this is occurring within the expression of your deeper loving qualities, and not simply for "bragging rights," you are supporting your work environment on both the level of energy and material achievement.

This is the best way to be recognized by others (bosses, co-workers, etc.), as it relates to promotion, compensation, and career advancement. The more emphasis you place on your inner wellness, within all facets of life, the greater your ability to function from this healthy place at work. This is a developmental process, so sincere intention, practice, and patience are required.

You are transcending your previous education in ego-control. Therefore, this path and process will vary for each of us depending upon the level of delusion we currently hold as truth. For those of you on the enlightened path, seek the elevation of consciousness that will shift your perspective, leading to more joy and appreciation for your truth.

Many people grow up believing that the world is filled with corruption and hardship, and that you must manipulate, intimidate, and abuse others in order to get what you want. Or, on the more subtle level, you simply turn your back on those in need. You've learned that what you "should" want most is wealth, security, comforts, power, and prestige.

While functioning within this mindset at work, you expect and require other people to sacrifice themselves and consistently do things for your benefit. When you don't get the treatment you think you're entitled to, you feel hassled and unsupported, jealous of what others have, and greedy for more. There is little, if any, joy and satisfaction in this experience of life.

Instead, once you accept the value of service, Unity, and a broader definition of success, you are much further down the enlightened path. It is more natural for you to be accountable for your own wellness, and to offer your best contribution for the benefit of all. You are far less hindered by the notion that others are out to get you, or take away your opportunities and achievements.

Career success is to a high degree intrinsically developed and recognized. Since we work with other people, in a marketplace that is fraught with competition and comparison, we may easily lose sight of the greater goal of joy, fulfillment, and wellness. You might be number one in your company or field of endeavor, yet if you have sacrificed your health, life balance, and connection to the internal qualities of joy and satisfaction, what have you really gained?

This brings another point to mind. Our joy and satisfaction at work go hand-in-hand with these qualities outside of work. This is where a more holistic view of your life is critical to the success of any single aspect of life. A home life filled with drama and suffering will be a great distraction and hindrance to any definition of success at work. And yet, if your entire fulfillment comes from your work, this is unsustainable to the joy and satisfaction of a healthy life balance. Therefore, endeavor to create the inner conditions that support joy and satisfaction within all areas of your life.

Regarding your work experiences, you will want to employ wisdom, mindfulness, and personal accountability – the tools for enlightened living. Wisdom comes from shifting your perspective to a higher truth. You are here, in this life and this job, as a spiritual being having a human experience. Therefore, elevate your perception of what is possible when aligned to this truth.

Develop your ability to be present more often in order to function from your place of Divinity instead of ego. Express loving energy leading to the manifestation of experiences that offer more cooperation and support. Be mindful of your ability to choose this, even when you experience challenges from others or from within. This will lead to inner wellness and guide you to a higher outcome.

And, as always, you are accountable for this transformation. It starts with the choice to be empowered enough to awaken to a higher perspective, regardless of what you believed about yourself in the past. This takes courage and inner strength – qualities inherent to your spiritual existence. Then you will develop your awareness and empowerment through intention and practice. You must navigate the rocky passage of unconsciousness and ego-control.

In utilizing these tools within your career you will experience greater joy and satisfaction in all matters. And in the times when you feel knocked down, you will more quickly pop back up, and re-align with your deeper truth. Always endeavor to recognize the joy and satisfaction in your work, this will greatly support Career Fulfillment!

CHAPTER 18
Surpassing Vulnerability

"Do not be too timid and squeamish about your actions. All life is an experiment."

- Ralph Waldo Emerson

A Challenge within the Human Condition

Can you think of a better reason to be here having your human experience on Earth, than for deeper healing, growth, service, and evolution? However, these rewards do not come to us as a natural consequence of merely surviving our life; which at times can feel like quite an achievement. And yet, it is this adversity and challenge, both within us and amongst others that potentially leads us to awaken and ascend to fulfill our higher purpose.

We spend our lives searching for our path, in order to both accomplish our ultimate destiny and navigate this physical existence. Accordingly, as our human life takes precedent, we may not be consciously aware of this spiritual journey. Yet, it is our truth none-the-less.

From our ego perception we most often recognize this quest as a struggle, with substantial opposition. We take our very first breath from the most vulnerable state imaginable, and then we fight to stay in this world against all odds. I suppose that this reflects the nature of identifying with a temporary experience and state of being. Of course, our higher identity knows of the greater goals founded in our permanence. To me, this suggests our need to integrate our spirituality into our humanity, for the greatest results.

In order to promote our best wellness and value, our two identities (Spirit and human) are meant to co-exist within this temporary experience. And not only co-exist, but flourish. Yet until we can understand and facilitate this truth in our everyday life, we are divided and at odds with our true power. And this internal conflict leads to outer frustration and even suffering – both individually and collectively.

While accounting for our unique differences, we each seek security and control as self-protection. We learn and endeavor to create an environment that shelters us from most anything that exposes our perceived weaknesses. In many instances this is a good and necessary aspect of our survival.

However, while survival is the ultimate goal for a human, as a spiritual being you are not susceptible to death. You are connected to a Divine energy that exists beyond time and space, so ultimately, survival is really not an issue. Therefore, the higher goal is healing, growth, and ascension of the Soul. This part of you knows that you have chosen the conditions of your human life for purposes that may transcend your human comforts and understanding.

The Nature of Vulnerability versus Growth

Within this context, your career provides an ideal opportunity to integrate your spirituality into your humanity. This is because, while your work is designed to provide the material sustenance needed for survival, it also opens the door to your spiritual fulfillment. Hence, the true meaning of Career Fulfillment; it supports your purpose of growth, service, and ascension. This is an enlightened view of your true career potential.

Career Fulfillment

Your fulfillment becomes about balance and integration. Regarding your involvement with work, when you are overly controlled by ego, you are inclined to hang on to what you know – to what is most comfortable. And if you are unhappy with your job or work conditions, what you know best is to feel and express frustration. This is the easiest path toward expressing your fearful energy, yet instead of improving things it more often keeps you stuck in negativity. From this place you are not honoring your truth or effectively serving others.

However, as you are willing to shift to your spiritual identity and honor your inner truth, you become empowered to take steps to grow and evolve. This is both the transcending of your vulnerability and the acceptance of your power and purpose. It is the highest expression of your energy within your human experience.

Based in the realization of your self-love, self-trust, and value, the result is the releasing of enough of your ego to explore the opportunities and possibilities that exist beyond the known and the "comfortable." I am calling this – "Surpassing Vulnerability." This is the elevation in consciousness that leads you to prioritize your growth and higher fulfillment over your delusional need for security and emotional protection.

At times we all will face our vulnerability, whether we like it or not. It's better to go into this space while intentionally creating your best life. Otherwise, for the sake of your need for growth (which always exists), your fear will "hunt you down" and force you to deal with your challenges from a position of weakness. You came here to heal, grow, and evolve, and you cannot hide from that responsibility. So, do your best to face it head on.

You must facilitate a certain amount of inner healing and the elevation of awareness in order to do this consciously. I am not talking about facing vulnerability through recklessness, impetuousness, or thrill-seeking. This is not based in love, which is the key requirement for personal and spiritual growth and wellness.

When connected to your inner wisdom through mindfulness you may become aware of a thought, feeling, or action that in some way represents growth and ascension for you. While controlled by ego you may reject or shy away from this idea in the guise of self-protection. However, within your spiritual practice, evaluate this further. Is your objection simply generated by the fear of change, failure, the unknown, criticism, etc.? If so, you may need to push through this fear in order to expand your best energy, and achieve your greatest fulfillment.

The truth is that we often receive signs from our Divine nature that is meant to guide us toward expansion, service, and contribution. But in this redirection from our familiar path we may succumb to our strong feelings of fear – our vulnerability. Yet, as your inner wisdom is showing you the path, allow and acknowledge your vulnerability. Know that your greater opportunity is to fulfil your purpose of growth, in that moment. Be resolved through inner strength to push through the fear, and do it anyway.

We all would like to know how things will turn out – in other words we want to control our experiences and the outcomes. However, this is not a part of the design of your human life. This is why I really like the quote from Ralph Waldo Emerson at the beginning of this chapter – life truly is an experiment. And you don't reach higher realizations and experiences without exploring new things.

Recognizing that there is a balance involving objective analysis and simply taking a chance and stepping into the unknown, continue to develop your inner wellness that is based in wisdom. Discover your unique path and purpose, and address your areas of resistance (need for healing). Be excited about opportunities that scare you a little, but offer great potential for expansion and fulfillment.

Accept the present moment experiences that stretch you. You get to decide when and how you are going to step into that space of trust. Be responsible for prioritizing your growth.

Vulnerability and Career Fulfillment

So, you have an "intuitive hit" about trying or pursuing something new within your career. Oh, I don't know, like maybe you are leaving the security of the accounting profession to be an author and teacher. Or, maybe that's just me.

Within yourself it may feel quite risky, and yet very exciting. But you have to balance the potential of this change with your best objective analysis. Not based in fear, but in a sound assessment applicable to your specific and unique path. And this involves developing your inner preparation for outer service.

Just so you know, you should not expect a joyful acceptance or approval of such endeavors from most of the "well-meaning" people in your life. Surpassing your vulnerability is not only challenging for you, it is also scary for those who don't want to see you make a mistake or fail. Yet, your purpose is to grow and ascend, and when you pursue this while connected to your higher truth, there is no "fail." Remember, it is the journey that brings the greatest joy and satisfaction!

Even while life is an experiment, it is somewhat uncommon to take a real chance on yourself. Yet, in the end, it's the only thing that is truly fulfilling. Regarding the discouragement coming from others, don't be too hard on them. Your shifting energy is challenging their inner beliefs and fears. And, maybe they are brought to re-evaluate their own lives. You may be awakening their recognition of their own need for growth and ascension.

In truth, Spiritual Law is always in play. Therefore, when you are predominantly fearful and insecure about your shifting path, people will pick up on this, and reflect the energy of doubt and fear back to you within their expressions. On the plus side, as you gain more momentum and acceptance your own power, growth, and fulfillment, you will project this more positive energy outward. And others will then appear to more supportive to you. Once again, all of your experiences start with your own inner state of wellness.

Back to your work related perspective and conditions. Are you offering your best energy or are you holding yourself back? Are you developing yourself and creating the greatest opportunities for growth? In other words, displaying a willingness to accept more responsibility and improve co-worker relations. Are you able to shift your daily focus toward contribution for its own sake, instead of worrying about whose noticing or getting the credit?

These are examples of your willingness to release some ego control (allow the feelings of vulnerability) and then express and function within the higher energy of love. Much of our hesitancy to face vulnerability comes from our unwillingness to accept that our life will flow just fine, without us constantly worrying about the future and trying to control things. And a mistake is not life or death, it is merely an opportunity to grow and learn.

What if you are functioning within your highest capacity, yet your intuition continues to tell you that this job is not in alignment with your greatest fulfillment and wellness? Are you going to stay put and gradually allow your energy to be depleted until you have only disdain for your job? Or, are you going to recognize and honor your inner truth and begin to analyze and explore other possibilities for work?

This is not always easy. There is a voice of fear and doubt that wants you to settle for the known, as unfulfilling as it is. You will think of all the reasons why it would be foolish to give up a "sure thing." This is another way of choosing, "the devil that you know versus the devil that you don't." Yet, Spirit has no use for "the devil," as this is a concocted identity of ego, and not in alignment with your truth.

This is the Spirit versus ego battle that we continually wage, within ourselves and within this world. Ego wants survival and security, while our Spirit knows a deeper truth and purpose. Of course, you will address and balance both sides as best you can. Yet, at some point you must step into the unknown. You will risk what you have for what you are capable of creating; you will evolve. Therefore, fully embrace your challenges with your greatest focus, intention, and energy.

In the end, we do what we need to survive. But never stop listening to your voice of truth. And move into your space of higher consciousness with respect to assessing your opportunities and possibilities to heal, grow, and evolve. You are on a journey that requires the integration of your spirituality into your humanity.

This leads to your greatest fulfillment, wellness, and success. This, however, is unattainable while you are unwilling to honor your truth. As you work through your process of inner healing and begin to surpass vulnerability, learn to "invest" in yourself (self-love, self-worth, self-belief, self-trust, etc.). The more you are able to do this the more your light will shine in a way that will inspire others to support your journey.

CHAPTER 19
Healthy Approach to Compensation

"Work to become, not to acquire."

- Elbert Hubbard

A Broader Definition of Compensation

I can hear this question ringing in my senses – "What about my compensation?" Let me ask you – is this the first thing you think about regarding current or prospective work? If so, you are not alone.

As someone who handled and managed the company's money and payroll for decades, I am well aware of this preoccupation. Not only the notion of getting paid as much money as possible, but also, making as much or more than "so-and-so." And before any consideration of their contribution or the financial status of the company, an employee will expect a raise.

We have learned to define "compensation" to mean the receiving of monetary reward (pay rate, benefits, etc.) from our job. Is this by far the most significant work factor for you? Are there other ways of recognizing compensation from your work?

Through my own experience and observation, I have noticed that overemphasizing your wages does not equate to a high level of fulfillment or achievement. And this single-minded pursuit is often short-sighted and not conducive to the success of the individual or the organization.

For the most part, our compensation in terms of pay is dependent upon the requirements of the job and the availability of funds to pay your wages. In other words, even while comparing the pay of similar jobs between companies and industries, you may find significant differences. This is due to profitability of the company, or otherwise a difference in fiscal philosophy. Typically, the payment of employee benefits (health insurance or other) falls along the same lines – type of position and financial ability of the company.

Many of you are working because you need money to live and to elevate the "quality" of your human life. When your focus is on your pay check, this most often means a desire to buy more expensive and luxurious things – house, car, adult toys, vacations, etc. Or, it could be a way of perceiving yourself as more valuable or important than others.

In other cases, your emphasis on pay may be motivated by the need to earn enough to simply keep a roof over your head and food on your table. Therefore, the motivation for, and sufficiency of compensation is relative. And I am not about to judge you, or suggest how much income should be sufficient.

Companies will always pay you as little as possible; that's just how it works. Yet, if you think that you will beat the system and make a huge amount of money owning your own company, you might be quite surprised and likely disappointed. Great personal demands are placed upon ownership, and the sad truth is that most businesses fail. In any case, financial compensation is important, and I am not saying that anyone should ignore this, or accept less than what their contribution should warrant.

Much of the consideration regarding how much we will get paid at work is a matter of economics. If you work at a job that is in high demand and limited supply, you are likely to be well paid. Maybe this position is very competitive,

Career Fulfillment

and requires unique natural ability and physical gifts, extensive education, or great skill. Prime examples are professional athletes or entertainers, medical doctors, CEO's, etc.

Most jobs fall into the "other" category – fewer prerequisites and less compensation, due to a greater supply versus demand. However, in areas with depressed economies, just obtaining and retaining a job can be challenging and your level of pay will be impacted.

Now, one only needs minimal awareness to understand that this world does not support equality for all when it comes to wages. Some are able to attain higher jobs and wages through discriminatory and unscrupulous means. And this is evidence of our need to awaken and elevate the collective consciousness among humans.

On another level, while equal in Spirit, we have each come into our human experience to heal, grow, and ascend according to our unique qualities and purpose. Our paths will necessarily look and function differently. This is not a judgment on our human value, and it is never a cause to exhibit unconscious, egocentric behavior toward your fellow human.

If it is within your unique life path to perform work that earns higher wages (while still leading with integrity), than this is your truth. No need to apologize for this, you are fulfilling your path. Accordingly, you will have more disposable income and a higher budget for "wants" and luxurious possessions. Yet, within your higher consciousness, you also possess a great opportunity to serve and assist others in need.

Otherwise, if this is not the case for you, your life path may lead you to work that is authentic, yet offers less in wages. You still are called upon to serve and contribute your best in order to achieve fulfillment. However, your opportunity to spend beyond your needs may be limited. Yet, these are the conditions from which you may still create a meaningful, balanced, and happy life. It's just that your emphasis will lean more toward the things that money can't buy.

All of that to say, the opportunity for equal and higher pay does not exist as an absolute for all in this world. Therefore, it is imperative for us to broaden our definition of success, value, and abundance. Our compensation must include a measure of joy, satisfaction, and fulfillment within the PROCESS of our work, and not simply the money we are paid for doing our work.

Fiscal Enlightenment

My message is for you to consider the value beyond your pay as it relates to your joy, satisfaction, and fulfillment. If you can shift your focus away from the things or lifestyles that are clearly beyond your grasp financially, you will create instant advantages. First, you will avail yourself to more work opportunities because you are less committed to only finding jobs based on rate of pay.

Secondly, instead of simply working hard for the money to barely cover (or fall short of) your bills, you will find less stress and more of a cushion for unexpected expenditures. And third, you might even be able to save some money for the future or some special purchase. As you are able to claim your value apart from your money and possessions, you will find a greater ability to live within your means in a joyful way.

Next, assess and consider the overall quality of the job and work environment as a part of your compensation. The quality and conditions may either feel like they add or detract from your wellness, and therefore, this represents value. In my accounting career some of the better paying jobs often came from companies with unreasonable expectations and understaffing, or domineering bosses/ownership.

Would you take less income to work within more satisfying and supportive conditions? I would. There are often many other factors to consider, such as, your connection to co-workers, work load and hours, commuting distance, travel requirements, sufficient tools or equipment, healthy and productive work space, etc. Look at all factors, not just the money; there is often a price to pay as a cost to your holistic wellness.

Even though your energy and spirituality is pervasive in all things, I am primarily talking about human conditions and circumstances (beyond your pay rate) that are more or less satisfactory. You need to define for yourself what is tolerable or intolerable, and what is supportive or unsupportive to your overall wellness. Yet, beyond any of the material attributes, with awareness, you will feel on the level of energy that which is aligned with your truth and purpose.

From the perspective of higher wisdom you can shift within your human experience to recognize personal value (joy and satisfaction) from your job. This is a more conscious approach than to simply pursue prestige or the luxuries that your salary can buy. What I know for sure is that picking a job entirely for its pay, simply because we have overextended and overcommitted ourselves financially, is ultimately a bad bargain.

Even if the "American way" has been to always desire bigger and better (whether you can afford it or not), resist this unwise practice and apply a more enlightened view. Pick the job that best suits your enjoyment, satisfaction, and skillset. Perform to your best, and earn pay increases as they become available. But live within your means – this is financial responsibility – coming from an enlightened accounting perspective.

Emphasize Your Work Contribution

In addition to considering an expanded view of your compensation, focus your energy upon how you may offer your best contribution. Here are three strong reasons to pursue this approach. First, for the intrinsic value it offers you, as described throughout this book. Second, because it is most supportive to the success of all others (the group, company, society, etc.). And third, it is the most effective and authentic way of generating career advancement (financial and otherwise).

Promoting wellness and value at work is a critical objective leading to career fulfillment. You are likely to contribute more to a job that you enjoy, rather than one that simply offers higher pay. And, you are more likely to enjoy a job that supports and honors you on a higher energetic level. Therefore, true success is more sustainable as you align your work with your Authentic Self.

Another significant personal benefit that does not immediately translate into higher income is the value of work/life experience. By taking a longer-term view of your work as the fulfillment of a deeper purpose, you know that it brings the experiences and opportunities that you need to heal, grow, ascend, and honor your truth. You contribute because this affords the greatest value for YOU, as well as others.

This is where your emphasis on the process of work is ultimately so much more valuable. "Career" is not a get-rich-quick scheme, from a more enlightened perspective. The real value to yourself and the world comes in the quality of your intentions and performance at work. This will certainly require a great shift in mindset and values for many people. Again, this is an awakening to a higher truth and wisdom.

Unfortunately, many employees have made it all about what they can get instead of what they can give. Within your higher identity, this is intrinsically unsatisfying.

Career Fulfillment

How much can I make here? When and what is my next raise going to be? How quickly can I get promoted?

This behavior represents the energy of your ego-nature. And when unchecked, it obscures the wisdom and loving energy that supports your true power and purpose. You may think that you are getting ahead, but within, you are disconnected from your truth. And ultimately, this will bring a level of inner suffering.

We have established our value and rewards in the attainment of worldly success (money, title, power, prestige, etc.). And too often our business leaders have exemplified this delusion. We have been taught that if you want to play the game you have to continue to abide by those rules. Of course, this greed and selfishness exacerbates the disparity in a world and financial system that makes it harder and harder for so many people to survive.

Therefore, how invigorating and inspiring would it be to work for (or run) a company filled with people who are more focused on what they can contribute? How much more enjoyable and supportive would this be for everyone? How much more successful and productive would your company be? Wouldn't more people be excited to wake up in the morning and go to work, anticipating all that they can accomplish?

Imagine if success was a thing that could be shared and not hoarded. Each team member contributes their best effort and skill. And accordingly, each is considered as valuable and worthy of proportionate compensation. While you cannot directly cause your co-workers to elevate to this higher perspective, you do have the ability to awaken and evolve yourself.

Your greatest evolution will come from being more conscious (less ego-driven) and loving at work. This is because it so directly impacts your holistic wellness, and Unity. Your primary focus must be on service and contribution, rather than the selfish pursuits of money and power that has corrupted our financial system and led us down this delusional and destructive path.

You can take the initiative to be accountable for your own energetic space which is concerned with offering your best gifts, qualities, and passion. When you emphasize your contribution and support of others, there is no need for comparison or competition that diminishes anyone's value. You are endeavoring to do and give your best with integrity and purpose.

I will dive into this much deeper in Part III, however, this is a key factor that allows you to view and approach your work experience beyond your pay check. Finding a deeper value is ultimately more satisfying and lasting, especially within the context of a balanced overall life. Contribution serves your spiritual purpose, and it leads to a healthier approach to compensation and Career Fulfillment.

PART II: Exercises

1) Whether you are attempting to get hired to a new job, or focusing on your performance within your current job, what are the inner qualities that you can bring to enhance your situation and support greater fulfillment at this time?

2) What are some specific steps you can take in order to create a healthier work/life balance, and more effectively manage your time? How might you shift your perceptions in order to realize more joy and satisfaction in doing your best at work?

3) Consider your current work relationships (co-workers, bosses, customers, etc.). With respect to those that seem to be most challenging, meditate upon the quality of the energy you are feeling about them, or expressing toward them. Knowing that only you can change your perspective and create your own wellness, discover how you may show more consideration and cooperation, or communicate more impeccably. Otherwise, how may you release the negativity within you, and simply accept them as they are?

PART II: Affirmations

I AM expressing my greatest loving energy in pursuit of my best job.

I AM now expressing my greatest loving energy within my performance at work.

I AM creating and promoting wellness within my happy, balanced life.

I AM now making the most effective and efficient use of my time.

I AM creating loving, supportive, and fulfilling relationships at work.

I AM offering my best contribution and cooperation at work.

I AM now empowered to communicate impeccably at work.

I AM now experiencing great joyful energy in the fulfillment of my best work.

I AM transcending my inner fear and vulnerability, leading to my healing, growth, and ascension.

I AM in alignment with my greatest fulfillment and satisfaction at work.

I AM grateful for all of the abundance that my career provides.

PART III

WISDOM IN SUPPORT OF CAREER FULFILLMENT

"When you are inspired by some great purpose, some extraordinary project, all your thoughts break their bounds. Your mind transcends limitations, your consciousness expands in every direction and you will find yourself in a new, great and wonderful world. Dormant forces, faculties and talents come alive, and you discover yourself to be a greater person by far than you ever dreamed yourself to be."

- Patanjali

PART III: Prologue

As you progress through your career and life, you have the opportunity to assess and understand all that you have previously experienced or witnessed in the world. And you can choose to awaken to a higher level of awareness and empowerment with respect to identifying and accepting your unique path and purpose. With this wisdom you may now apply the tools of mindfulness and accountability in order to create your most authentic success and fulfillment at work.

In this final section I will offer specific lessons in higher wisdom that may support career fulfillment for you. Within your various stages and career transitions you would be wise to apply the inner healing and growth that you have developed within your spiritual practice. As you elevate your consciousness, you may transcend the feeling or belief that work is a negative place or concept. You move from simply tolerating it as an unwanted chore, and ascend to the higher potential and purpose to be fulfilled.

As you walk your most authentic path, you know that you are uniquely qualified and authorized to contribute your best gifts, qualities, and passion. You will apply impeccable integrity as you offer your best service to the world. And it is this enlightened perspective that actually offers you the greatest joy, peace, abundance, and fulfillment from your career. Through your highest consciousness, always seek to add your light and love into the world, for the benefit of all.

PART III: Energetic Quality or Tool

As you endeavor to bring wisdom into the creation and experience of your most fulfilling career, the energetic quality or tool most beneficial is *LOVE*. So, what does this mean? The Divine quality of love is expansive and inclusive; it opens a path for healing, growth, ascension, and service. Love is the source of wisdom, which is most supportive to a higher definition of success and fulfillment. And wisdom is a key ingredient in the application of enlightenment at work.

The opposite or conflicting energy is *FEAR*, which is restrictive, self-centered, and self-protective. When immersed within this lower energy at work, we disconnect from both our source of power and our supportive energetic attraction with others. We fall prey to the delusion of our ego-nature. Fear narrows our perspective and discourages us from seeing our highest potential, and that of other people.

Love, which has largely been defined as a fantastic romantic notion, is actually the energetic quality of your true existence. Therefore, this is a deeper connection that touches and elevates us to identify with our Authentic Self, and that of all others. It is for us to accept and recognize the potential in this quality for our own healing and transformation, and in support of our greatest wellness and fulfillment as humans.

CHAPTER 20
Career Wisdom – Discovery

"The only way to do great work is to love what you do. If you haven't found it yet, keep looking. Don't settle."

- Steve Jobs

Inner preparation for outer service is a life-long endeavor, and the more that you honor this approach the greater your opportunity for sustained success. Even while it may take different forms at different stages of your life and career, the enlightened position is to always connect to your Higher Self in order to live authentic and empowered. You are to learn or re-learn your truth within the power of each present moment. This is how you evolve and continue to honor yourself and others. As always, apply the three keys to enlightenment – wisdom, mindfulness, and accountability – in your work and all things.

We each awaken, evolve, and reside within our own level of consciousness according to our need for inner healing and our deeper purpose to be fulfilled. Since this varies from person to person, my purpose is not to try to define your path for you. Instead, I will offer wisdom that may relate to the typical needs and growth patterns common to many people at various career stages. I am expressing my truth regarding a higher perspective that may be helpful to you. As you recognize your truth in this wisdom, then develop the intention of applying it into your circumstances.

Enlightened career strategies are about fulfilling a greater contribution and purpose. This transcends merely getting and tolerating a job in order to pay your bills. Even though we all have experienced this circumstance from time-to-time; just know that you have a purpose of creating a deeper satisfaction and fulfillment. You are uniquely qualified and authorized to contribute your best gifts, qualities, and passion in the work that you do. Yet, this must be an approach that you consciously and continually intend, create, and nurture.

The Discovery Stage

I am calling the initial stages of your career "The Discovery Stage." This initially takes place in early adulthood as we begin working full-time. And it even applies to our intentions in college, once we are purposefully focused on a field of study relating to career options and interests. It also will certainly relate to any significant transitions.

Within this process you may be relatively unsure of yourself, inexperienced, and maybe a bit intimidated by other people. On the positive side, you may be more energized, open to learning, enthusiastic, and committed. While these are all natural reactions, there are healthy or destructive ways to deal with this.

First of all, and it cannot be overstated, the better prepared you are within, the more capable you will be toward transcending the challenges and creating success. Often, we think that it is about our knowledge or experience. And to the extent that these bring greater confidence and self-trust, these are valuable. Yet, ultimately you realize that these are moving targets; you are continually learning and having new experiences.

Therefore, from a more enlightened perspective, the biggest hindrance to your success in this stage comes from your inner fear and need for energetic healing. Your level of self-love, acceptance, and relative connection to your present moment power is what is most supportive. The greater your degree of inner wellness, the more likely you are to just step in and be content in giving your best effort. There is less self-judgment leading to self-doubt and power struggles.

From wherever your level of consciousness, this is where you will begin your new journey into this career phase. Regardless of this, we all typically enter an environment that is new to us and requires that we learn many things. This "learning" will impact you on an inner energetic level, as well as, your outer work experiences.

While bringing your previous levels of experience, technical knowledge, and education, this still may be insufficient regarding this transition. Within whatever training process your employer administers, you must get up to speed and improve your ability to do the job for which you were hired. What my experience has taught me is that most employers are woefully lacking in both the organization and training methods that would be supportive to its new employees.

Therefore, you would be best served to understand and accept the requirement of your own accountability. Choose to take the initiative for your learning and otherwise assimilating into the culture and expectations of the job. Never assume that anyone else will take responsibility for your progress, wellness, or success. Entitlement is a concept of ego and not Spirit.

The more "unconscious" the organization the more isolated you may feel. This is typically an environment that fosters an abundance of "self-interest," especially at the top. So your greatest strategy is always to develop your own inner strength through a higher connection to your truth and loving energy.

While on the job, learn the keys to doing your tasks to the best of your ability. If you find a lack of support from others, do not become despondent or lose your confidence.

Find your strength and value in your effort to serve and contribute your best. Be creative and persistent, yet humble and cooperative. These are inner qualities that support outer service. Accept the challenge as part of your ongoing growth.

Take the initiative to ask for guidance and assistance in order to be more effective in your job. Learn to encourage others to desire to help you. They are not obligated to do so. Therefore, always present your highest, healthiest, loving truth. Be self-sufficient, open, helpful, and kind, as you express your inner-strength in a positive way. And, of course, always show appreciation when you receive their support. This is how you nurture the higher energetic qualities and relationships at work.

On the level of energy, this stage brings new stimulus, as you integrate with the energy of your co-workers. From this standpoint, you don't know exactly what you are walking into when you start a job. Some environments will be more conscious and loving than others. In any case, your focus and accountability for your inner wellness is critical. This is not a selfish principle, because your wellness leads to your best output.

To the extent that you are merely adjusting to the job and not overly concerned about being validated by others, you are miles ahead of the game. Additionally, you are wise to accept other people as they are. You are not there to label, change, or complain about them, you are there to offer your best energy into your work situations and relationships. Be respectful of all, regardless of title or position. Ultimately, this is a reflection of your inner wellness, not theirs. Allow others to be impacted by your light, without expecting them to notice.

For many people, this Discovery Stage can be quite challenging. Instead of living in our power, we allow our inner fear to make us feel vulnerable, in which case our ego charges in to defend our image or attack others. Your inner preparation leading to healing and growth is incredibly significant to your success. You are expressing and engaging your energy within the fulfillment of your higher purpose, in relation to your work.

This is why it is essential to your career fulfillment to align with your highest values and focus on your service and contribution. Moment-to-moment and day-to-day you are exerting great effort (energy and time) in order to accomplish the goals of the job. Sometimes you will feel "in the flow." Everything is clicking and you easily feel satisfied with your production, interactions, and results.

Of course, at other times you will feel lost and defeated. You may not grasp what you are expected to do, and on top of that, you might feel rejected or embarrassed. Yet, even while people are not exerting their influence in a supportive way, your job is to rely on the truth of your inner strength, value, and purpose.

When controlled by delusion your ego will run wild and create problems energetically. It is common in this career stage to exhibit an inferiority complex. This is inner fear (ego) that may manifest itself in one of two ways. One, you are overly shy and self-conscious as you are hard on yourself and afraid to make a mistake. You retract your power and self-confidence by deferring to others with the assumption that they are "better" than you.

Or two, you have the same inferior beliefs, but you take a more assertive position of showing a false strength, which may be seen as arrogant, aggressive, or confrontational. Within your best energy you don't have to cower or boast. Accept that you are in a new situation and learning, and that doing your best is all that you can ask of yourself. In work and life you are always in process, so give yourself a break.

Ego-control leads us to the expression of negative energy based upon two routine outcomes. When things go our way we may be overly-inflated and obnoxious; or when we make mistakes and feel inadequate, we become depressed or angry. In other words, we are falsely finding our value in how we think we appear to others, and are expressing our energy from this source of inner fear. And then, within this delusion we define ourselves as successful or unsuccessful. Either way we are creating inner suffering based in delusion.

In truth a single moment should never define you; it only signifies the energetic quality within a moment of experience. From there, a choice to shift to a higher state is available from the perspective of love. Learn to be humble in achievement, and calm yet strong in times of difficulty. All of your experiences are opportunities to facilitate further healing, growth, and ascension.

In the early stages of your career you are likely to have a greater variance of "good or bad" experiences than once you are more established. This is just the learning and expanding process. So a key strategy in this phase is to focus on the reward and value of your PROGRESS – intentionally recognize the things you are doing well, instead of over-emphasizing your mistakes, deficiencies, or results. Even if other people seem to be doing better, your path is not their path. And they likely had their own struggles within their learning curve.

On the enlightened path you will rightfully pursue progress not perfection. Never expect that you should be the first perfect human. When you can subdue your ego in the present moment of a fearful expression, you can recognize greater peace, patience, and self-love. Within this empowered state you will learn from your experiences and develop compassion for yourself and other people.

CHAPTER 21
Career Wisdom – Developmental

"Strive not to be a success, but rather to be of value."

- Albert Einstein

The Developmental Stage

In truth, if we are living our fullest life, every day is "developmental." Life is always in-process. And therefore, with respect to career, I am classifying this on-going pursuit as the "Developmental Stage." Within this phase we have at least advanced past the beginner phase and are now attempting to establish ourselves within some higher level of skill and understanding.

As we become less focused on "proving" ourselves to others, we become more focused on independently recognizing our own sufficiency and worthiness. Rather than pacifying our ego, our goal is to offer and add greater value. Our intentions are to continue on this career path, even while this may lead to a change of our position or employer. Hence, even as we are now a bit steadier, we still want to challenge ourselves to improve both our career and life standing.

Development is synonymous with growth, a purpose that we all share while choosing this human journey. This requires a balance of controlling what is within our own understanding and power, and accepting and adapting to new challenges and opportunities. We build our platform through our integrity and consistent effort. And then, while standing upon this platform, we begin to create the next level of our development. Within this incremental growth we find inner fulfillment as we improve our outer contribution.

As always, in order to maintain your energy and fulfill your highest path you will certainly need to focus on your inner wellness and connection to truth. It is easy to either become complacent, or stray down the wrong track, once you have transcended the initial challenges of your work.

At some point, your ego-based nature is likely to look for the path of least resistance. And when this leads to stagnation (or simply "defending your turf") it no longer serves your purpose of growth and ascension on the spiritual level. Your work then becomes less satisfying and fulfilling.

Your goal must be to create and experience the greatest fulfillment from your work, which is supported by your greatest contribution. Regardless of your job, you are serving others in some way. And with intention you can express your best loving energy and share your gifts with enthusiasm.

The other path is to do the least amount of work possible, in order to continue to get your paycheck. This can be the dynamic that many will encounter within this stage of their career. Holding on to what they have, too afraid to risk growth. Know that this is a choice, but not a satisfying result.

I have seen and experienced this myself. My background has involved office settings, but I am sure this relates to all types of jobs, especially those that are not strictly based upon income production (sales/commissions). Most companies are severely lacking in the application of objective "measurable's" that may be used as a criteria to determine one's productivity and effectiveness.

Therefore, they are reliant upon the integrity of the worker and the effectiveness of management. Will the employee continue to give their best and remain engaged in their work? Does management have the required capability and desire to monitor and support their staff? These are real business issues that only work well with higher accountability, integrity, and contribution

When you are functioning connected to your elevated energy and purpose you will internally generate and express greater integrity and do your best for its own sake. However, from time-to-time you may lose this connection, because of personal life challenges, apathy toward your job, difficulty with bosses or co-workers, etc. At this point, while on the enlightened path, you must recognize your responsibility to make some changes for the sake of growth and fulfillment.

If you are unaware or unwilling to facilitate this shift, you may find yourself in a steady or rapid decline. When this happens you will likely be in for a more dramatic event to foster your awakening. Ignoring the signs of dissatisfaction, and lack of energy or interest, creates the conditions where your job will spiral downward until you are fired or forced by others to change your energy and attitude. Therefore, rather than complaining and commiserating with other unhappy (unconscious) co-workers, be mindful of your highest purpose at work and take the steps to regain your best energy without the need for great outside disturbance.

Your highest level of inner wellness will keep you interested in both contribution and achievement. This advancement may encourage you to elevate to more responsible positions, whereby, you may be line for greater rewards. Seeking higher compensation as a result of greater contribution is a noble attainment.

This is different than expecting a raise without real merit. Therefore, your greatest career success comes from integrating your spiritual qualities into your daily functions at work. Focus on offering your best service/contribution within an awareness and connection to your deeper truth, and then expand your energy as a path to greater human rewards.

Within this Development Stage of your career it is wise to assess your inner motivations and level of commitment on a somewhat regular basis. As you are able to expand your consciousness you will occasionally be reminded or provoked by the existence of any disturbance to your otherwise peaceful, loving energy.

Determine if this is due to some temporary disruption or if there is a more pervasive energy that would require significant action. The goal of enlightened living is to maintain this deeper awareness and alignment so that you are able to make the appropriate adjustments before there is a substantial problem.

Maybe you need the challenge of a new job (within or without your current company) in order to facilitate growth. As your energy becomes too stagnant, you may be guided to change something – small or great. I have witnessed countless people who, based upon their energy and satisfaction at work, should have addressed this for themselves years ago. This is highly unsupportive to their well-being, and it deteriorates the healthy energy within the company.

If you decide to stay in the same position but recognize a need for growth there are options. The first thing is to become more present. Focus your mind toward a greater awareness and appreciation of each task as you do it. **This is the essence of mindfulness**.

It keeps you energetically connected to the quality of your work. Otherwise, being primarily unfocused gives your mind too much time to dwell on what you don't want or like. On some level you are wishing for something better without expending the effort, courage, or self-love to create it.

Next, if you determine that you are proficient and effectively present in your current job, you may decide to focus more energy on supporting others. With the higher goal being contribution, you can express yourself as a valuable "team member" by assisting others in some way with your positive energy.

Rather than choosing to expand to a more responsible and higher ranking position, you may expand the depth of your service within the position you currently hold. You might spend more time training, assisting, encouraging, or counseling co-workers as a way to find greater personal fulfillment and to elevate the energetic capacity of others. This is a higher path leading to personal rewards while honoring your integrity.

Of course, to bring further challenge to this stage of career, we often now have our own family and financial responsibilities that will require our energy and attention. This is where life balance and time management considerations are most advantageous. You cannot control other people or external events, but with wisdom and practice you can greatly affect your inner state of wellness, to minimize the many self-generated and self-inflicted problems most people create.

Once again, as with the earlier stage of your career, you must be willing to face vulnerability. This is a reminder to keep going and growing. It is the expansion of your energy into uncharted territory that challenges your inner fear – yet your ascension and fulfillment requires it.

Learn to accept change as good, and to balance the known with the unknown. Trust the inner wisdom (intuition) that comes from your Authentic Self, and follow it. Your greatest development comes from honoring yourself in this way, rather than talking yourself out of following your own truth. While applying this spiritual principle into your career, you will create the greatest value, fulfillment and success – for yourself and others.

CHAPTER 22
Career Wisdom – Realization

"If you follow your bliss, you put yourself on a kind of track, which has been there all the while waiting for you, and the life that you ought to be living is the one you are living."

- Joseph Campbell

The Realization Stage

This phase typically encompasses the latter portion of your established career, and reflects greater maturity connected to your work. Yet, through the application of higher consciousness you don't have to wait until you are older to have this experience. Advancing through your career mirrors your advancement in life. It happens through your awakening to a higher truth, and not simply the passage of time.

Your work is merely an extension of who you are. Whereas, your primary career focus may have previously been about "ambition," the new mantra is, "I am now focused on creating more meaning in my life." Your attitudes, motivation, and effort now shift to be more supportive of others.

Within your career – are you evolving? Are you exhibiting greater wisdom in the choices you make? Are you more appreciative and aware of the things that are most important?

Have you developed greater self-awareness that supports Unity? Are you able to be more focused on contributing to the wellness of others? And, are you more often adding into the world your light and love, or your darkness and fear?

Within your career, are you growing and finding ways to engage your deeper interest and passion? Do you appreciate the blessing of satisfying and fulfilling work, as an opportunity to continue to serve and be relevant? Do you treat your co-workers and associates with kindness and respect, which comes from a deeper acceptance of the value of others (regardless of their status or position)? Are you representing yourself by expressing your best loving, peaceful, and joyful energy, which may assist, guide, and inspire others?

All of these queries and considerations are significant to your holistic wellness and relevant toward experiencing more meaning. The embodiment of these higher principles is attainable; and not simply "new-age" cliché. While *On the Enlightened Path*, this represents the best intention and practice, of which you are fully capable. It is the culmination of your moment-to-moment application of wisdom, mindfulness, and accountability.

Will you experience this same level of wellness and Unity simply by following your usual ego-controlled fearful delusion, and the desires and opinions of others? No. You are to continually evolve within your highest intentions, practices, and purpose, as you shift toward greater fulfillment on your life path.

Let me clarify what I mean be "latter stages" of your career. Typically, you have spent a significant amount of your adult life working in your chosen profession. It does not necessarily mean that you are nearing retirement age. It's just that you are now seeking a level beyond the previous stages of discovery and development – you are moving into the deeper meaning of realization.

Career Fulfillment

Realization translates as, "A state of understanding or becoming aware of something." In the context of this teaching, I am applying this "understanding and awareness," to the deeper, truer principles of your existence. And this should, at some point, manifest into your career goals.

Within a course of ascension, this should be the stage of your career when you recognize greater value in all that you do – in all that exists. Therefore, it can be stated that not all people will achieve this stage in their lifetime. If you are not following an enlightened path of ascension, you may simply find yourself burnt out and worn out. You may just be "coasting" to the end of the "race."

Maybe you have become unfulfilled and severely unsatisfied with your stagnant energy and work/life experience. You may even falsely believe that all would be fine if you simply made more money. But, your purpose is much deeper than that. You have seen it and done it a certain way for many years, and you might be anxious and fearful of changing, adapting, or learning anything new. Maybe your plan is to just hang on as long as possible while you are waiting to retire, or be pushed out the door.

This is an all too common circumstance in the workplace. And when this happens, the older employees are jealous and judgmental of the younger people; while the younger employees have lost respect for the older ones. It becomes an unproductive power struggle.

With any amount of attentiveness you will notice that many people are less than fulfilled at work. Can you clearly see that this adds little or no value to your life or that of the others around you? Even if change is difficult, with a higher level of understanding and awareness would you not be more inclined to pursue it?

While we all reside in our own unique conditions and characteristics, to a large degree, our willingness to shift to a more enlightened path is a matter of choice. We can choose to continue to grow and contribute as long as we are alive. What are you choosing for your career and life?

Sometimes people hit this plateau earlier than others, maybe forties or fifties; way too early to think about simply retiring. Therefore, it is for you to recognize your authority and responsibility to assess your inner energetic wellness and guidance. Ask yourself: How do I rekindle my passion? What is my passion at this stage of life? What are my current opportunities versus responsibilities?

The natural flow of energy dictates that we change, and that life changes around us. And without it there is no evolution or real contribution. Therefore, what was chosen as your path and purpose earlier in life is likely not your best alignment now.

Can you see that your perspective based in the intention of self-preservation is no longer supporting your greatest wellness and fulfillment? This energy will manifest primarily as fear, boredom, anxiety, dissatisfaction, selfishness, judgment, even illness. So maybe you are simply holding on to your job because you believe that there is nothing else you can do, and you need the money.

None of this makes you a bad person, or even uncommon. It is, however, evidence of being controlled by ego, fear, and delusion. And this is not honoring your personal healing, growth, and ascension.

My purpose in writing this material is to inform (remind) you that there is a higher path and perception that is much more fulfilling and satisfying within the context of your work and career. As you are able to notice yourself within the lower energy forms detailed above, you may decide to facilitate some changes.

Begin by shifting and expanding your belief system. Know that you are capable of serving and contributing in ways that are just waiting to be discovered. This will literally bring you back around to the Discovery Stage. With wide-eyed enthusiasm you will receive a new and powerful energy. Yet, unlike earlier in your career, you now have greater wisdom through life experience, and don't scare so easily.

Making this shift and transition takes persistence and inner preparation, as you are overcoming engrained mental habits steeped in limitation. Yet, it is within your control to shift your perceptions, to be more empowered. More than a possibility, it is your purpose.

You start, as with any efforts for healing, growth, and ascension, from the inside out. Intentionally connect with your own higher truth, whether through meditation, prayer, or other forms of inner inspirational focus. Ask the questions that are most relevant – and be patient for the answers. If you are open, your intuition may reply quickly. Try to notice your truth before ego tells you why it is "impossible" or "too difficult or risky." Learn to trust your higher wisdom.

There are various options within your career path that may elevate your interest, passion, and fulfillment. You may determine that a whole new career path is most beneficial and in alignment with your truth. This could take the form of self-employment or as an employee in a new company or industry.

Or, you may recognize a new opportunity within your current profession, something that will cause you to learn and expand in powerful ways. Finally, you may find your fulfillment in some form of charitable work or hobby. For most of us, there is something we always wanted to do or share with others; this may be your best time to pursue this dream.

There is often great vulnerability as you open to changes that involve your career. It not only challenges your perception of self-worth, but often times your very identity. Always take into strong consideration your basic needs for financial sustenance before leaving any job.

Yet, there is great benefit in learning to recognize your value beyond your job title and the comforts of your habitual life. Be courageous but not reckless or impulsive. Understand your overall obligations and responsibilities. Significant career changes must be coordinated within the context of your life as a whole. This is to be a holistic process of ascension.

You may need to continue your job while planning (and saving money) for this change. Or maybe you are required to work part-time while you develop your new opportunity. Be smart, be patient, and be thorough. You are not looking for a quick and easy fix to spice up your life.

You are realizing your true inner wisdom that is guiding you into alignment with your gifts, interests, and passion at this stage of your life. You are reconnecting to your higher edict of meaning and fulfillment through a renewed intention and effort. *You are following your bliss.*

My Work Transition

This is the stage of career in which I found myself recently. I had spent thirty years in various accounting - management positions within numerous companies. I was fifty years old, part owner and a Vice President for a small health insurance company. I had woven my way through this unique career, and was now beginning to recognize a level of dissatisfaction and depletion of energy and enthusiasm.

My compensation was fine, but it could not offer fulfillment on a deeper level. This work certainly served me in the past, yet I no longer could mistake it for my passion. I was able to remain productive, and retain my position, until the most appropriate time to transition to something new. We sold our company, and although I had the option of staying on at my executive management position, I knew that it was time for me to go. And, even with the loss of income, I never looked back with regret. My focus was on love and expansion, and not fear and security.

Within previous career stages, and levels of consciousness, I would not have been able to make this shift. However, while in alignment with my higher truth, I knew that my joy and fulfillment required a new path. I was willing to sacrifice certain things in order to elevate the inner quality of my life – I was willing to bet on myself and a higher purpose/identity.

Again, I was far too young to stop working, and while I appreciate the funds I received from the sale, they were not enough to support me for too long. So, I chose to maximize the financial results by minimizing my living expenses, which gave me a window of time to pursue my dreams unencumbered by other work. We always have choices, especially when our values align with our purpose.

Within my inner assessment I recognized that my greatest joy and fulfillment always came from immersing myself in spiritual principles and wisdom that have a practical application. I loved to study it, discuss it, and use it to support my own well-being, and to guide and assist others as the occasion arose. I never quite knew if or how this could become my profession, yet the first step was in recognizing my passion.

The next step, as it turned out, was to begin to shift my mind (and ego) to begin to identify myself as something other than my previous professional title (accountant in my case). This was surprisingly challenging. Even transitioning out of the habitual practice of going to an office every day was very odd. I am not looking for sympathy; I am simply describing that you will have to learn who you are without your usual job and habits. And, you will have to develop greater independence toward defining your value, and discipline regarding the proper use of your time.

Once I got some space from my old work identity, I began to take actions toward planning and developing my new career. This started with creating the conditions for inner wellness, and then moved to include an outer focus on what I want to create and how I will proceed. Regarding career pursuits, this initially caused me to try some independent work. There is often some exploration and growth that ultimately leads you to further define your path. This then, helped me discover writing, teaching, and mentoring.

My development is always ongoing, yet as I am able to honor my true wisdom I have been able to quiet the voice of ego (fear and doubt). You will be challenged within when you display the audacity to envision a higher path. Part of you wants to retreat to the known. Yet, as you endeavor to live in the present, it is your ability to choose love over fear that keeps you going.

As much as possible, even while having a general long term vision, my focus has been on my production, joy, and fulfillment in the present. This is where my power lies, and therefore, I have a measure of control. My focus on the future tended to place me into the unknown, which at times created the return of fear and anxiety.

As of the time of this writing, it has now been five years since I left my previous career. In that span of time I have published four books, I have taught community college classes, and I have mentored individuals. This is a good start, and a significant transition. From the standpoint of my overall business, I still consider myself to be in the Discovery Stage.

I recognize my new career as a long-term developmental process. I am doing the work that I love, and as I am ready within, the opportunities that are in alignment with my energy and purpose will present themselves – in the right way, place, and time. I am open to any outcome, because I am living my joy and truth in the present.

Additionally, I have adjusted and coordinated my life to best facilitate this significant change in my career goals. I previously had a salary that afforded certain lifestyle options. And now, without this salary, I must adjust my living conditions accordingly. Admittedly, this was not as difficult for me as it might be for many others. I find my joy and prosperity in my inner wellness and peace, as opposed to the things I can buy. But in any case, it is essential that you live within your means, or according to a well thought out budget.

My path and purpose is different than yours – no better or worse – just different. Whatever you have always wanted to pursue, there are principles in wisdom that are most supportive to your fulfillment. You do not have to write or teach spirituality and holistic wellness in order for this to be true.

However, recognize your passion and inner motivation for taking these career steps. In order to be sustainable and to achieve the higher definitions of success, you must be driven by a deeper calling or pervasive purpose to serve. And this must be in alignment with your unique gifts, values, and life path.

Summary

If you will notice, I am teaching that there are cycles, which align with your inner personal development, that coincide with your career. You start out more excited and passionate about discovering new things and you seek to be recognized in a positive light by others. As you move down the path a bit, you may gain greater confidence in your ability to survive in the world and offer quality work. Through your ambition you may focus heavily on achieving a higher status and income, and eventually you may have the lofty title and pay that you desire. But is this enough?

As you ascend in life you may recognize a shift from ambition to meaning (as Dr. Wayne Dyer says it in his book called, *The Shift*). You may begin to more deeply consider what is truly valuable, and realize that it is your purpose to find and live your truth.

As you continue to move along your career path you need not get stuck in your disillusion and disempowerment. You may choose to honor yourself by creating new avenues of energy that support your growth and wellness. Hence, with renewed passion and enthusiasm you are invigorated. In some ways you will recycle back to the phases of discovery and development, yet you do so within the realization of greater wisdom and meaning.

You are now focused on offering your best service with integrity in order to contribute your light and love into the world, in whatever way is authentic for you. Your time may be seen as more valuable, as there is less ahead than behind you. Therefore, the true higher purpose of your career becomes more evident and easily accepted. Utilize your time and energy in the way that suits your brand of inner wellness and fulfillment – this is most supportive to the world.

CHAPTER 23
Leading with Integrity

"Successful people are always looking for opportunities to help others. Unsuccessful people are asking, what's in it for me?"

- Brian Tracy

The Quality and Nature of Integrity

Integrity is an essential quality for fulfillment and true success. It is the principle of doing the right things for the right reasons. You do your best in any given situation because that represents the most empowered and loving you. On the enlightened path this is supported by living within your true higher identity as often as possible.

This is the connection to your Authentic Self, and the integration of your spirituality into your humanity. *Meriam-Webster* defines integrity as, "The quality of being honest and fair;" and, "The state of being complete or whole." Thus, integrity is an inner quality of truth and wholeness, a clear representation of the deeper Divine energy within you. Therefore, it is a way in which we express unconditional love for ourselves and others – the preeminent quality of Spirit.

Of course, we all have heard about living this way. Virtually all world religions were founded upon these principles handed down by enlightened Masters. This was before their words and message were re-directed to support some power struggle within humanity. So, since we are aware that this is our higher path, why is this not the energy most often exhibited and expressed in business and in the world?

Why is leading with integrity so often quite challenging and conditional? In truth, we all face the contradicting energy of fear, coming from our ego identification, even while we desire to live from a more elevated position. Therefore, it takes a specific and on-going intention and effort to rise above our fear and selfishness. It takes an awakening to the higher truth and potential available to us within our human experience.

As we function from a lack of higher awareness and identity, our expressions of pure integrity become an unnatural state. In fact, at times, the very objective of offering your integrity may be considered naïve by others. It's a pretty sad state of affairs when offering integrity, compassion, and cooperation is taken as weakness. Welcome to the ego-nature of humanity.

Many people will question the necessity of integrity as integral to career success. They may say, "While it's always "a good idea," when push comes to shove you better fall back to ego protection." What the world generally has considered to be "successful," renders standards like integrity somewhat obsolete and unnecessary.

Being judged as having more material prosperity or power than many others has become the accepted definition, regardless of how you got there or how much joy, peace, and fulfillment it brings you. Therefore, you don't need to have integrity to make a lot of money, wield significant power, or be the envy of the masses.

Certainly within the context of work and business, love and integrity seems like extraneous concepts. Competition has been king. Kill or be killed, one man's ascension is another man's demise, and profit at all cost. Manipulate and discriminate if you must, the end justifies the means. In the land of ego, many have been enriched materially, while being bankrupt spiritually.

This lack of emphasis on integrity has created the chasm and disparity that exists in our country and world. It prevents goods and services from being shared and offered to the benefit of many if that means minimizing the profits of the few. And it eliminates opportunities for many to participate, contribute, and prosper from career service.

Clearly, for the sake of your holistic wellness and the betterment of all humanity, you must begin to function within a new, higher level of consciousness that represents a more enlightened path. It starts with individuals courageous enough to expand their perceptions (minimize their ego-based delusion) and dare to lead with integrity. This is especially powerful when done by those who exert greater influence in business – Owners, Managers, and other leaders. But even within your own sphere of impact, you can help to shift the culture.

What is most important for me to share is that you don't just lead with integrity in consideration for others (though this is part of it). In truth, it is also YOUR best path to personal fulfillment and wellness. You are not abandoning your personal needs, or denying your potential for achievement. You are honoring yourself to a higher degree, which supports all aspects of your existence.

And many times, even while shifting from selfishness to integrity, you will still end up within an experience of life that includes worldly success that is authentic for you. But your journey will be more loving, peaceful, and connected to your higher truth. You are building and living upon a stronger foundation that will support you (and others) through the changes and ups and downs of life.

Have you noticed while driving your car, when someone will race by you, only to be abruptly forced to stop at the next light? You may think, was all that aggression, selfishness, and lack of respect for others (and the law), really necessary or worthwhile? In fact, they did not get to where they were going any faster.

In this example, they are functioning with a lack of awareness and power in the present moment, and solely focused upon their personal needs, desires, self-importance, and some future destination. They are missing the opportunity to be more conscious of all that exist around them. And, they are risking their wellness, while forfeiting their own peace and satisfaction. Many people constantly live in this delusional space.

Yet, on a more enlightened path of integrity and awareness you are present and conscious of your thoughts and actions. Your awareness considers not only your value, but that of those around you. You each have needs, desires, and goals that are equally important. Within this example, you are driving the speed limit, steadily progressing down your path, staying within your peaceful but productive nature. You will likely get to where you want to be just as fast, yet, you are more capable of enjoying the journey. Plus, you have not harmed anyone in the process.

I am not declaring those who lack integrity as evil, sinful, and wicked. To my awareness, there is no point in labels that devalue us. We are all in need of awakening, healing, and aligning with our higher nature. When we express energy that lacks integrity – to whatever degree – we must realign through wisdom, mindfulness, and accountability.

Whatever ways and methods of functioning that were accepted and pervasive in the past should not be the criteria we use in choosing our path today. There is no elevation in consciousness without progression. What matters most is gaining awareness of when we fall short, and as a priority, recognizing this as an opportunity to shift our energy toward more loving and empowering expressions.

Your integrity is for the benefit of all beings, including yourself. You cannot fulfil this principle of unconditional love only when it supports your own ego (beliefs, comforts, popularity, etc.). It's time to transcend our false and fear-based habits. Awaken to your possibilities while living a higher path that fulfills both spiritual and human wellness.

Integrity at Work

Within the daily activities and considerations of your work, strive to align with the higher qualities of integrity. This is evidenced by your intentions, motivations, and personal effort. Always strive to be honest, sincere, considerate, compassionate, earnest, and supportive – because it is ultimately the best you can do for yourself and other people. It is, therefore, the right thing to do. Of course, this originates from your expressions of love, according to your state of inner wellness.

All of the principles of energetic healing start with your inner space. From there you will express your level of wellness (or lack thereof) outwardly. Therefore, healing-transforming your inner fear and delusion is the only way to elevate your ability to lead with integrity. Ultimately, we can only share what we are. Do you want to share your loving nature, or your selfish, fearful ego-nature? This is more than an intellectual decision.

When I am happy and healthy I naturally want you to be happy and healthy. When I feel peaceful and prosperous, I will act in ways that support these qualities for you as well. Yet, when people are insecure and unhappy within, they will project this energy to others. While controlled by their ego they will have a very difficult time accepting and encouraging your best loving and successful experience. This is just the nature of energy.

Instead of working openly and honestly with others, we might consider them a threat to us (our job, beliefs, survival, lifestyle, etc.). We wrongly believe that our success and wellness is controlled by others, or that their success diminishes ours. Therefore, we feel justified in helping ourselves to whatever we want, no matter the cost. Or, we easily condemn others as bad or wrong, in order to elevate our self-image or status. And by the way, we all succumb to this weakness, fear, and delusion from time to time.

For many, this behavior has spelled worldly success. Therefore, its transcendence is a tough thing to promote. We are required to take a bigger picture view of the consequences of our individual actions. This only happens when we intentionally strive for the higher path that supports our inner healing and wellness.

Integrity requires that we look at our own life, and determine where we can be more influential for the good and wellness of all. It is not about being perfect; it is in the sincere striving for integrity that we succeed. You may function with more integrity than so-and-so, yet, this is not the standard. It is not a comparative-judgmental thing. You must elevate to your highest integrity and wholeness – for your greatest reward.

As we choose to elevate our human experience by offering loving energy to all, we also elevate the consciousness in the world. But since we can only affect this within our own life – in each present moment – we must trust in a higher purpose, process, and wisdom than that which has been taught and followed by the masses historically.

Regardless of your specific job, there are countless opportunities where you can lead with integrity. Even while it is true that your energetic state varies, it remains your intention to notice your thoughts, feelings, and actions through mindfulness. Then you may adjust and realign to your loving energy as often as you can. Only you can know when you are honestly giving your best efforts, based in unconditional love.

Career Fulfillment

Your level of consciousness and motivation will be a key factor in the quality of your attitude and expressions. Are you doing the minimum simply to avoid scrutiny or worse? Or, are you conscious of doing your best and going beyond the requirements? Are you acting one way when co-workers are watching and another way when you are alone? Are you as productive as you can be? Or, are you wasting time on the internet, personal smart phone, chatting with others, etc.? How deeply do you care about the quality of your work or the success of your co-workers (or the company)?

When you are leading with integrity you are empowered to stand in your own truth. Regardless of how you may be judged by others, you can be confident and satisfied that you are doing your best. Plus, through your integrity, you will continue to grow, ascend, and be a positive example for others. While it may require patience, in a very authentic and organic way you are fulfilling your unique purpose. And you will be noticed, appreciated, and rewarded by those in a position to support you. This is how you create career fulfillment and success by leading with integrity.

CHAPTER 24
Contribution Brings Greater Rewards

"I determine to render more and better service, each day, than I am being paid to render. Those that reach the top are the ones who are not content with doing only what is required of them."

- Og Mandino

Contribution Leads to Success

The greatest focus within your career must be on CONTRIBUTION! This leads to your highest internal and external rewards. Apart from the established standards of performance that may exist for your job, contribution is more about your inner motivation and integrity.

When you shift to a higher value and effort at work, you will treat your work as a deeper calling. You are leading with integrity, which means that you are offering your best effort and intentions in alignment with your true higher identity. This is how you were designed to function; this is the realization of your true potential.

Just to be clear, contribution is the edict for career fulfillment. However, your higher life goal involving holistic wellness (love, joy, peace, health, service, etc.) indicates a proper balance of your energy within all aspects of your Being.

Therefore, contribute your best while at work, yet, make sure that you are not sacrificing your overall life balance and wellness.

Once again, this is an example of integrating your spirituality into your humanity, for the greatest benefit of both. Doesn't it make sense that when you offer your best energetic expressions (thoughts, words, feelings, and actions) connected to your work, you are naturally better positioned to contribute higher value? I hope that you can see that you are then living within a higher degree of wellness and fulfillment that is intrinsically rewarding.

This level of involvement creates the experiences that encompass the greater definition of career success. Consciously choose to heal and grow within, and intentionally select your career path according to your unique gifts and purpose. Then, offer your love, joy, and passion to the tasks that comprise your daily work regiment.

Your ongoing enlightened process will be to enhance and maintain your inner wellness in order to string together days, weeks, months, and years within this higher application. Add to this your willingness to honor and support your co-workers and associates as a part of fulfilling your work responsibility. Would you not agree that this defines higher contribution?

So then, what are the rewards that such a level of contribution may bring? As with any expression of integrity, you know that this represents your connection to your Authentic Self. And therefore, first of all, this higher level of functioning is its own reward.

How much more empowered are you when you live your truth? You give your best as a reflection of the best within you. This not only elevates your energy, but it minimizes the proclivity to "follow the crowd" and choose the lower path of ego gratification without concern for the consequences.

Next, as you contribute to your highest level, in addition to spiritual wellness, you create the optimal conditions for your work related success. Your best efforts to do your job well and to support others within a common goal, becomes the very recipe for the success of the organization. Even while you can only control your own efforts and intentions, you are still creating the energy and results that encourage a positive outcome.

Because of your priority for contribution, you are intent upon earning your rewards based upon the quality of your service and work. As this creates the greatest benefit to all, you will be best positioned to receive the appreciation that brings material reward as well. This, of course, provides an opportunity to improve the quality and conditions of your personal life.

Contribution Leading to Growth

Another reason for offering your highest contribution at work is in the area of personal/spiritual growth. While giving your best with integrity, you can assess your career path in the light of higher truth. Therefore, you are giving yourself the best opportunity to realize your hopes and dreams within your career aspirations.

You can now evaluate the external conditions objectively in order to determine if your best is in alignment with your desired conditions and fulfillment from work. How do you connect with the current direction, capacity, and integrity of those you work with or for? Are you still passionate and inspired to contribute your best? Do you still recognize opportunities to grow, improve, and contribute more? Use your inner connection to gain awareness of your answers.

It is my contention that your level of contribution is a greater motivating factor for success and fulfillment than your financial compensation. High contribution sustains your interest and success regardless of your income. Still, while focusing on contribution, you will be in a position to evaluate your pay to determine if it is appropriate based upon the market place and your personal needs. If you decide that it is not, your growth and success will open doors to new opportunities that may adequately support you in this way.

Otherwise, (as was discussed previously) the path for those who are primarily unconscious (self-centered) is to function first and last with a focus upon their salary and benefits. Sometimes this attitude at work represents a sense of false entitlement. However, it is also probable that this is evidence of a lack of value or interest in the actual work. In either case, you will not adequately serve or grow. This is a slow (or fast) track to complacency and dissatisfaction.

For these individuals, enough is rarely (if ever) enough. They are trying to fill the whole within by adding external rewards. This is an equation that cannot work. Their motivation disproportionately emphasizes receiving over giving, which is not intrinsically rewarding, and only really creates inner stress and outer conflict.

Ultimately we are not fulfilled by our bank accounts or the things we may purchase. It's not like winning the lottery, which is a one-time event that may cover your bills for life. Your work requires that you show up and fulfill your duties daily. Without the right focus or mindset, this can quickly become a grind and an exercise in dissatisfaction. Therefore, the only sustainable definition of success is to learn to create and realize the inner joy, purpose, and fulfillment from the actual work.

Contribution Leading to Enlightenment

There is a path or progression to enlightened living and higher consciousness. Examples are, inner wellness and preparation leads to better outer service; and higher contribution leads to greater rewards. We are spiritual beings having a human experience, and not the other way around. Therefore, the pursuit of human wellness and success requires our initial focus upon accepting and expressing our greater inner qualities and identity. Then, we may integrate our Divinity into our humanity for the best results in support of wholeness and Unity.

Our moment-to-moment practice in choosing to apply wisdom, mindfulness, and accountability is the key to self-mastery. When we can choose to love and honor ourselves in this way, we become the masters of our life. And we greatly benefit others while gaining great inner rewards.

And when we fall into the trap and habit of ego-control, we temporarily disconnect from Spirit and create conditions that are more challenging and less satisfying. Our focus has shifted from contribution and meaning, to personal gain and ambition. Utilizing wisdom and awareness, you must guard against this attitude and behavior.

From an enlightened perspective, this is not too difficult to understand. However, we must awaken from our delusion, and develop ourselves for this higher loving service. In case you didn't notice, your life experiences have been teaching you this wisdom all along. No one can do this work for you, which is why I find accountability to be so critical to enlightenment.

The moment-to-moment intention and effort to live within your highest connection, supports you in offering your greatest contribution at work. At times this will flow more smoothly than other times. This is where your wisdom and mindfulness are essential.

Whether you may be feeling a temporary lower energy within, or whether some person or external situation is disturbing your energy, you simply must recognize this as your present reality. Now, face it honestly and take responsibility for shifting your perceptions and making any necessary changes to reside in loving energy. You are contributing to your wellness.

Your focus is always on doing the best you can, and elevating your energy through awareness and self-love. This should support you in choosing the actions that are most healing to you at the time. Maybe you need a break or extra rest. Your body works in concert with your energy, so learn to listen to what it's telling you. Or maybe you need to confront a work situation with honesty and courage. Often times we feel more stress by putting off some unpleasant business than actually dealing with it.

Also, when your focus is on contribution and doing your best, you can learn to remain unattached to the toxic energy of others. You can accept that while your best may fluctuate from day-to-day, you are offering all that you can at the time. When this is true, you can always live with the consequences. The perception, opinion, and lack of consciousness in other people is their business not yours. Learn to develop and honor your own inner strength, this brings a strong measure of peace and wellness that is another example of greater rewards.

CHAPTER 25
Applying Self-Awareness at Work

"If you can channel the best part of you that is bigger than yourself, where it is not about your ego and not about getting ahead, then you can have fun and aren't jealous of others. You see other people's talents as another branch of your own. You can keep it rooted in joy. Life is long and there are plenty of opportunities to make mistakes. The point of it all is to learn."

- Ethan Hawke

A Tool to Support your Truth

In the previous chapters I have emphasized the wisdom of leading with **integrity** and focusing on **contribution**. This brings an empowering energy and perspective that naturally leads to achievement and wellness. You are more assertive within the expression of your authentic truth and inner strength. Whereas, spending too much attention on external rewards, recognition, and approval, is the sign of insecurity coming from your lower energetic state.

Awareness is defined as: having or showing realization, perception, or knowledge. As this relates to your own personality and life path, you have **self-awareness**. Within a spiritual context, this relates to your true self – your Authentic Self; as opposed to your lower nature – your ego self.

Along these lines, **self-awareness** is the antidote to unconsciousness (detachment from higher truth) and delusion (persistence within your lower ego-based beliefs). It's a great tool for supporting your own success on both a spiritual and human level, and as a path to Unity Consciousness. You are empowered to take a more direct path to your success without harming others.

Integrating your Divine qualities into your humanity does require some balancing. The first key to self-awareness is to gain a deeper understanding of your truth, value, and purpose. This was addressed heavily in Part I.

Regarding your career, you have your own unique path to fulfill. Your work or service is a higher calling, a way of sharing your gifts. Yet, if you undervalue yourself or otherwise hide your gifts from the world, then you are not fulfilling your destiny. Therefore, you are not on a path of higher self-awareness or career fulfillment.

As you learn to trust yourself, the balance part is in deciphering when to be more assertive in speaking and acting upon your truth, and when to accept and allow a situation as it presently exists. You are always both coordinating with others and creating your own path. Within the bounds of integrity your intentions are pure, yet, even when standing up for yourself you must be aware and mindful of the impact upon you and other people.

Self-awareness guides you to take the actions or speak the words that are most supportive to your transcendence, growth, and ascension. Self-awareness requires your presence, and views your experience from a higher perspective. Without this quality you are likely to create personal and professional challenges and conflicts rather than enhance your fulfillment and honor your truth.

If you find yourself in any situations where you are being mistreated or dishonored, you must take the appropriate steps for your own well-being. Through self-awareness, you may adamantly and mindfully work to develop your self-love and self-respect. Connect to your deeper truth (identity, value, and purpose), as a reminder of your potential for inner strength.

Be empowered to speak your truth with impeccability, and direct your path toward that which is more supportive. The goal is to honor and elevate you, rather than focusing upon the egotistical behavior of others.

At times we are asked to do something above and beyond, that requires extra effort, skill, or both. You may feel that while your production clearly enriches others, you are not receiving adequate consideration, compensation, etc. Accordingly, your ego may create a great internal struggle.

Do you do all that you are asked to do, and simply trust that others will recognize and reward your value and contribution? Or, do you balk at and complain about this potential inequity? This is a very real dilemma for many people in the business world, and a situation where your self-awareness and higher consciousness are to be utilized.

When you can go to the place of your deeper connection, apart from the delusion of your ego-mind, what is your truth telling you? Is your focus primarily upon service-contribution or external rewards? This is where a view toward balance is beneficial.

What does your awareness tell you about the way that you and others have been treated by the company or boss in the past? Do you feel that they primarily lead with integrity or not? What is the impact to you if you do this work to your best ability? Are there ways to express your concerns openly with your employer? If satisfaction is not possible, is this an issue that would compel you to leave the company? If so, what would be the next step in your career?

Your focus upon greater self-love will compel you to both do your best and support your highest wellness. A focus on ego/fear will lure you into the withholding of your best effort, and create self-doubt about your value and purpose. And it will negatively affect your perceptions of others, and theirs of you.

Notice how you are not being asked to blindly follow the will of other people. I am teaching that through self-awareness you will have a clearer perception of your truth, and therefore, will be more empowered to take the actions most supportive to you. This becomes a very proactive approach to dealing with work issues of all kinds.

Along with taking this inner journey through self-awareness, there is another critical step. You must become very mindful and present with your energy (thoughts, words, feelings, and actions). In this case, you will deal with "what-is," and eliminate the "what-ifs."

Deal with reality and not conjecture. Create what you desire from the place of reality and truth. Now you may apply your inner knowing to the situation at hand, rather than anticipating problems that don't really exist. This is the essence of mindfulness.

There is no complete assurance as to how others will treat you, and therefore, I am teaching you to move beyond your ego's desire for such. As part of self-mastery, your self-awareness is a tool to keep you connected to your inner knowing – intuition. This is information from a higher level that is available to guide you.

Since all people function within their own perceptions, values, and self-interest, everyone feels justified in acting according to their delusion. Learn to accept that others will contradict you in this way from time-to-time. Your job is to persist in honoring your inner truth, while allowing other people to live in theirs.

When you choose to do this from a position of self-love you will be accountable for listening to your truth and taking the steps you are guided to take. You may be led to offer greater patience while continuing to observe the unfolding of a situation; or you may be guided to communicate your truth impeccably and take some further action. In any case, trust yourself, and therefore, be more at ease regarding any consequences. This is how you consciously create your best life and career fulfillment.

However, when you descend into your ego you will function within the energy of fear. You may ignore your intuition, or talk yourself out of this knowing. You feel powerless and at the mercy of the others involved. You're distracted from giving your best effort or offended that you are not "given your due."

Either way, your production and satisfaction is impaired. Depending upon the magnitude of the situation you will eventually create the conditions of suffering within. This may lead to harming your relationships or quitting your job prematurely.

The quality or result of your human experiences is a bit of a gamble; uncertainty is your common companion. Therefore, learn to "bet" on yourself. But endeavor to do this from your space of self-love and not inner fear. To me, this is why it is so logical to focus more on your inner wellness, self-love, and truth, rather than be consistently swept away by the tides of delusion from ourselves and others. Through your self-awareness you learn to honor yourself in the process of sharing your light and love into the world.

Your best self-awareness will define your true purpose within career. This includes your overall aspirations, as well as your specific challenges that arise from time-to-time. Some of you will have a strong inner drive to lead others, promote innovation, improve existing standards, and assume greater responsibility. And, others of you will be content to create greater balance and wellness outside of the spot light, following the established program, and contributing your best within the defined tasks assigned.

No right or wrong, better or worse; simply a difference in gifts, qualities, passion, and purpose. Through self-awareness you will determine YOUR path. Career Fulfillment on the Enlightened Path is about honoring your truth and offering your best loving energy. Use your self-awareness to remain in your wisdom, strength, and self-love, as you navigate the various experiences that arise at work.

Being versus Doing

Based upon the qualities and purpose of our unique life path, I find that some people are more naturally attuned toward **"Being,"** while others prioritize the **"Doing."** Yet, as a way of honoring your highest potential, self-mastery requires an adequate balance of the two energies. Neither is good or bad, just potentially incomplete. One is more inner-oriented and the other more externally expressive.

How you utilize and balance this energy is quite relevant toward obtaining what you want at work, and it reflects your level of self-awareness. You have an opportunity to learn where you need to grow and evolve. And, this will support you toward relating in a more understanding way with other people, who may typically function differently than you do.

We each have our own qualities and gifts, designed for the fulfillment of our highest purpose. Consequently, we should honor these traits. However, as we elevate in consciousness, we must endeavor to incorporate divergent energies that offer improved balance. This leads to greater fulfillment, service, and contribution at work.

Therefore, those inclined toward the more introverted "being," will utilize self-awareness to develop the ability to more easily express their inner truth out into the world. People who identify as extroverted may find the "doing" to be more natural. Yet, they will need greater self-awareness and inner reflection in order to access and connect with their higher truth. In doing this, they may direct their expressions and interactions in a more loving way.

The "Being" part of this process involves connecting with the sacred aspect of you that knows your truth and deeper purpose. This is a great thing to develop in meditation, prayer, or other solemn setting. You must be willing to endure and thrive in stillness; something that "doers" may find quite challenging. It requires that you be completely honest and objective with yourself. Your motives are pure. And your integrity is wrapped in self-love and inner strength.

This process is less reactionary and more contemplative. However, with self-awareness it need not be a drawn out ordeal. With practice, you may be able to make this connection rather quickly in order to respond to a more active, fluid, or volatile situation.

The "Doing" that is required in the human world is what is most often noticed by others. Your actions, words, and interactions are constantly on display. Yet, it is the energy that is directing this outer activity that is most critical. Some "doers" are loud, aggressive, and demonstrative, while others are more low-key. In any case, you are either expressing the energy of love or fear. This will tell you whether you're "doing" is adding light or creating darkness.

Within the realm of "doing," you have a choice, but only when connected to your Authentic Self. Your actions may represent great love and joy, cooperation and Unity, and impeccable communication that encourages and supports you and others. Or, you may simply lash out from the fear and delusion that reveals your need for an awakening toward inner healing and growth.

So, for those who have been gifted with great energy toward outer activity, appreciate this quality. But know that it is your responsibility to guide and direct this energy from your place of consciousness – higher identity, wisdom, and mindfulness. Invest in your process of inner healing, growth, and ascension. Even if this initially feels like "inactivity," it is a valuable use of your time. Your evolution requires that you gradually develop and connect to your power from your higher Source.

In doing this, you have the potential to accomplish great things in service to the world. Additionally, you will develop the inner love and strength that is most fulfilling, and your best path to wellness. Your light and powerful energy is needed in the world today!

If you are someone who more naturally connects to your best energy from within, be grateful for this tremendous gift. You are a conduit to the Divine. This higher understanding may support you in offering great love, peace, and Unity.

However, your evolution involves your willingness and ability to leave the comforts of your own space. You may have a natural fear of the delusion and unconsciousness coming from other people. Yet, you chose this human journey which necessitates that you participate in this world. Therefore, you must intentionally seek opportunities outside of yourself, in order to positively impact the world. Develop your "doing" in order to effectively serve and contribute in your career.

Whoever you are, and in whatever way you more naturally function – strive to be whole within your unique journey. As was said earlier, wholeness is an attribute of integrity. Therefore, offering your best integrity, contribution, and self-awareness at work will lead you to BE connected to your truth, while you DO as a function of performing your job.

CHAPTER 26
Career Growth and Ascension

"Success is not final, failure is not fatal: it is the courage to continue that counts."

- Winston Churchill

Your natural career progression is one of growth and ascension while fulfilling your purpose on the enlightened path. It is the continual process of offering value to others while honoring your own wellness and success. Regardless of how this manifests on the outside, it is really an intrinsic quality that we recognize within.

When you are focused upon the fulfillment of your inner truth and purpose, you will find the drive and motivation to continually offer and contribute more throughout your career. Wisdom and self-awareness will grow as you utilize your integrity to bring forth the loving qualities that support healing and transcendence over your challenges and disempowering beliefs of the past. This relates to both your work and personal life circumstances.

Then, as your delusion diminishes you are more sincere in your efforts and more selfless in your motives. You will assume accountability for creating your life, while releasing the expectation that others are responsible for your wellness.

If you are able to truly absorb the previous paragraphs, recognize that it defines a tremendous shift in the way most people are taught to perceive their lives and career. When you consider your own life and higher potential I hope that you can see that the pursuit of these qualities, intentions, perceptions, and actions are highly conducive to a happier and healthier life. To me, this is the purpose of true enlightenment within our human lives.

Your career growth and ascension is interconnected with your personal/spiritual growth and ascension. The sooner that you are able to bring your best personal energy, truth, and awareness into your life the quicker you will find meaning, balance, and fulfillment in your career.

Otherwise, we typically learn the need to shift our perception, effort, and energy after experiencing unsatisfying conditions that bring some form of suffering. It is always up to us. We are responsible for our own learning, healing, and growing, and within our own wisdom we may accomplish this in a more gentle and supportive way.

When I speak of delusion, I am talking of our mental framework, based in ego, which has us vacillate between notions of grandeur or self-condemnation. Are you great and entitled above others – No. Are you hopelessly incompetent and unworthy of success – No. Yet within a career focus where you compare and prioritize your rewards and accomplishments over your contribution and integrity, this becomes the mental delusion that imprisons you.

It is founded from insecurity and fear. In this way, you rob yourself of the joy, peace, and satisfaction available to you in each present moment. You are busy looking over your shoulder for threats, or worrying about how others may judge you. While you may still visit these extreme mental swings from time-to-time, your mindfulness is a tool for grounding you in your deeper truth. And, its consistent practice supports your sustained growth and ascension.

When your career growth leads to a promotion within your group, company, or industry, then honor and appreciate this result. Or, even when seemingly unnoticed, your growth leads to consistent, high quality work that supports you and benefits those around you, this is a great result as well. You cannot always "buy things" with your rewards, sometimes they simply translate into satisfaction and joy within. Since you have your own unique gifts, qualities, and purpose to fulfill, success always involves aligning with your truth and doing your best work.

A primary message in this book is that success, growth, and ascension is not conditional to any comparison with others!

All of our lives we have been trying to impress other people and seek their approval. Whether it is what we do, or how we do it, we have overly valued their opinions, and under-valued or own truth. This influence may come from family, friends, society, or the media. However, you must gain the inner strength necessary to define and follow your own career track. Otherwise, this is where we fall into the trap of ego, which then pulls us out of our truth and into judgment and inauthentic pursuits.

Our paths are not the same, and the playing field is not level for all; therefore, the conditions of our success and fulfillment are not the same. We are equal in value – as spiritual beings – while we are separate within our human conditions, path, and purpose. Our variety of career choices will rightfully reflect this diversity.

Please do not interpret anything that I am writing to suggest that you are to settle for less. I am simply offering that you each must determine for yourself what are your best effort, production, goals and objectives, leading to your definition of wellness, fulfillment, and abundance. You are to experience your career in alignment with your own higher truth. And, enjoying the process or journey as much as the result is a gift you give to yourself.

In fact, with self-awareness, I hope that you recognize that I am teaching the opposite of "settling." You are to honor the entirety of your Being. This involves recognizing and nurturing your full potential to do the work that is most joyful and meaningful for you. Believe and trust in yourself, and then be accountable for doing the inner and outer work to progress toward your goals.

Additionally, don't settle by sacrificing your inner wellness for money or prestige alone. To grow and ascend means that you are creating greater value, wellness, and fulfillment. These are inner qualities of energy that have nothing to do with money or "stuff."

If, while elevating your inner wellness you are also increasing your salary, then great. Yet, to sacrifice your health, life balance, relationships, and integrity, simply for more income, is a form of settling for less than you are designed to experience and attain.

Another form of settling is staying stuck in a job - to "plateau." In order to ascend, energy needs to expand. In whatever way this pertains to you and your career, you are to challenge yourself to give and receive more over time. This likely will require you to change and grow in some fashion. And, it will keep your work fresh, interesting, and fulfilling.

This may entail finding new ways to perceive and function within your existing job, or you may realize the desire to try a new job or career path. In any case, connect to your inner truth often. Recognize the quality of your energy toward your career, and then act accordingly, with the intent of fulfilling your goal of growth and ascension.

CHAPTER 27
Examples of Consciousness at Work

"The last of human freedoms: to choose one's attitude in any given set of circumstances, to choose one's own way."

- Viktor Frankl

I have written about the significance of being more conscious at work. In this sense, "consciousness" represents a connection to your deeper truth and wisdom, applied to the work/service aspect of your life. This is a very significant and advantageous position, which supports your perspective, intentions, and expressions based in the energy of love.

This quality of love must be integrated into your daily tasks and interactions, as well as, your overall motivations and aspirations. Even while this is a higher level of functioning, that supports your inner healing, growth, and ascension, it is also a greater path to career fulfillment. From whatever capacity you are currently functioning at work, know that YOU are creating your experiences, and impacting others. Your ability to offer your best presence and awareness in any given situation will elevate your experience and support of others.

However, while functioning within unconsciousness, your quality of energy is depleted, and a disconnection with other people is created. I will tell you that you must be consistently vigilant in maintaining your connection to your self-love and truth. Through years of false training and habitual thinking, we so routinely sabotage our energy and identity, and then return to expressions of fear and negativity. Therefore, your ongoing practice is to remain aligned with your own deeper truth in each present moment. This is the "self-mastery" about which I have written. And this is the great benefit of enlightened living.

The following items will help you determine how consciously and successfully you are aligning with your higher truth and loving energy in your career path:

(1) Do you feel joy in the process of performing your daily tasks?

(2) Are you able to appreciate a sufficient quality of peaceful inner space before you become concerned about the next task or day's work?

(3) Do you naturally and easily function at work from your best integrity?

(4) Are you able to focus upon your service and contribution as your greater meaning and fulfillment at work?

(5) Are you able to quickly detach (or not even engage) from the drama and negativity of others connected to your work?

(6) Are you creating value for the stakeholders (all of those connected to your work) within your sphere of influence?

(7) Are you continuing to challenge yourself to grow and ascend along your career path?

Career Fulfillment

Here is a brief description of the above items. In Chapter 28 I will offer guidance as to how they may be applied within three primary career classifications: Employee, Management-Ownership, and Self-Employed.

1) When you have consciously chosen your career path from the space of awareness of your best gifts, qualities, interests, and passion, you will more deeply and authentically relate to the value and performance of your job. Finding the joy in this work is an intrinsic quality. Even while you will encounter experiences that are difficult and challenging from time to time, the overall feeling around your work should be joy and satisfaction in the accomplishment of your daily tasks.
Otherwise, if you show up each day with indignation, simply tolerating the work for the potential material rewards, you are not approaching your career from love or consciousness. You must develop yourself in a way that supports a perspective, approach, and effort that creates positive feelings in the actual work.

2) If you become so overwhelmed by either the difficulty or quantity of your work expectations, the quality of your energy may be depleted rather quickly. Or, you may find these conditions to be utterly hopeless, and beyond your ability to ever "catch-up" or perform to the desired standards. Therefore, you must be accountable for creating more reasonable and supportive conditions.
In support of your wellness, you endeavor to recognize a sufficient amount of satisfaction and peace in a job well done, before the next wave comes crashing down on you. In order to accomplish this, you are required to change the way you

work, the details of the job, or the expectations of others. Seek within yourself for the answer and the most appropriate way to resolve this issue.

3) To be conscious at work you must routinely offer your best energy from a place of integrity. If this is a struggle for you, then you are likely in need of an awakening to a more empowered view of your truth and potential. You offer your integrity as an expression of your inner love; therefore, you may need to work toward connecting with your loving truth and releasing your attachment to ego/fear. However, you may be leading with integrity in all that you do at work, and find that this is not received positively. You may recognize that within the overall culture that other people seem to be ascending in the organization by means void of integrity. In this case, you may want to evaluate the appropriateness of this job for you.

4) Are you primarily motivated by the value you receive while focusing on your level of contribution, or on your expectation of material rewards? When conscious, you will find greater fulfillment by giving your time and effort toward the things that have intrinsic meaning to you. This connects you to your unique purpose, and reflects your self-awareness for creating career fulfillment. Within this wisdom, when you do receive material rewards, you do so with greater joy and appreciation. You feel fully worthy, knowing that your rewards rightfully followed your best service and contribution. Additionally, it is always wise to focus your energy upon the things you can create, rather than relying upon the whims and motivations of others.

Career Fulfillment

5) While functioning within a more conscious level, we create choices in the way we choose to express and behave, which would otherwise not appear available to us. When disconnected, we react from our inner place of fear, as we are confronted by the negativity of others. However, while you remain within a connection to your self-love and higher truth, you may simply observe the actions/words of others.
You need not immediately diminish your energy in order to attach to theirs. You then may respond in a way that more effectively honors your truth and theirs. Toward career fulfillment, your time is much better spent engaged in positive and productive energy, and while more conscious you are aligned with this capability.

6) While conscious at work you are aware of the impression and impact that your energy and service have upon other people. Through mindfulness you exhibit a higher emotional intelligence (EQ). Connected to your job you may have an impact on many stakeholders, such as, co-workers (team members), managers/owners, customers, vendors, and more. Understanding this potential for adding value or withdrawing it, you consciously choose to offer your best loving service for the benefit of all. You will find your greatest fulfillment as you work within this higher perspective and intention.

7) Your consciousness supports you in maintaining an awareness of your energetic expressions and contributions. Just like in a relationship, you must assess the quality and nature of your ongoing

passion and purpose. If your connection to work is not growing and evolving over time, then it is not leading to your ascension. And you will experience a loss of enthusiasm and fulfillment which will bring negativity and dissatisfaction within your life as a whole. Therefore, your career fulfillment requires that you continually challenge yourself to grow and evolve.

Based upon this assessment of your level of consciousness at work, how will you proceed on your enlightened path? Will you keep the status quo, while still expecting to elevate your career fulfillment? Or will you utilize this wisdom to shift and grow into a more conscious employee and human? As a way of offering your light and love into the world, for the benefit of you and all others, I hope that you will become more accountable for contributing and evolving.

CHAPTER 28
Career Classifications: An Enlightened View

"Outstanding leaders go out of their way to boost the self-esteem of their personnel. If people believe in themselves, it's amazing what they can accomplish."

- Sam Walton

Consciousness for Employees

For purposes of this discussion I am considering "employee" to be one who's primary function does not include upper management or ownership (they will be addressed later in this chapter). This comprises the vast majority of our population of workers. As an employee, other people are in control of what you are to do, and for the most part, how you are to do it. You go to work each day, handle your responsibilities as best you can, and then come home to your personal life.

Your continued employment and rate of pay are determined by management. While this apparent lack of control is challenging to some people, it is best for you to focus on the many things you can control. First of all, you always have the ultimate control, you can leave this work if you choose to; you are not a slave or indentured servant.

The primary focus of this book is upon creating career fulfillment and empowerment, coming from an enlightened perspective (through wisdom, mindfulness, and accountability). Accordingly, self-mastery becomes the key to your success. As you heal, grow, and develop within, you have tremendous control in how you choose to experience your work life.

So, you have a boss at work. This means that in addition to being accountable to yourself, part of your job is to fulfill the expectations expressed by this person. This necessitates a positive and effective relationship. In truth, when you are performing your work from a space of consciousness and offering your best contribution, your boss will likely be very supportive and grateful. This is because your success positively reflects upon them to their superiors.

To this end, always endeavor to lead with your highest integrity. Apply your best energy into cultivating mutual respect with your boss (and co-workers). Just by the very nature and truth that "someone" has a measure of power over you regarding your work, does not automatically mean that it needs to be a negative experience.

Peel back your ego to understand that you each have a job to do, and what is most important is that you play your role in support of the successful fulfillment of the work. You have the opportunity to both help yourself and them. They have the opportunity to help themselves and you.

Or you could choose to be disrespectful and plot to sabotage the other. Of what benefit is this behavior? And yet, while under ego-control we often embrace this negativity through our own fear and delusion. Instead, enlightenment guides you to work toward the success of all, because within, you realize your true value.

When you function connected to ego, you may think it oppressive to have a boss; someone to tell you what to do. And you may even harbor the belief that you are smarter or more talented than they are. Of what value are these judgments?

Career Fulfillment

They do not improve your relationships or support you in the higher performance of your work.

Through your intentions for service and contribution you will naturally show yourself to be smart, talented, and maybe, worthy of elevating to a management position. Let your contribution and integrity do your bidding. Otherwise, being obstinate, difficult, or disrespectful is a message to management that is unsupportive to your success.

There are many advantages in simply being an employee versus managing or owning a business. First, your primary focus can be on the specific requirements of our own job, rather than the work of others. And if you have been able to pursue and attain employment in a job that is suited to your unique gifts, skills, and interest, then you have the tools to find enjoyment and satisfaction in the performance of this job.

Next, because you are only responsible for yourself and your own work, you have a greater measure of control over your performance than someone who has to manage or supervise other people. Of course, you work with and for others, under varying conditions, which may affect the outcome of your work. However, since the duties of a management position includes being responsible for others, their focus is split. They will have less direct control over the quality and effectiveness of the work for which they are specifically responsible.

Another advantage is that as long as the company remains in business, and you perform your job well, you are likely to have employment. Therefore, you are able to focus on your job and let other people focus on the overall culture and solvency of the company. And when you leave work for the day, you may more easily release this energy and experience overall peace and wellness. This is a luxury that ownership does not always enjoy.

You are responsible for YOUR culture. In other words, you are accountable for your positive energy, integrity, productivity, and fulfillment. And with your best inner wellness, you have control over this.

Learn to respect all other people, regardless of their position. Whether co-worker or boss, they are just as human as you. They simply may have chosen a path of leadership at work. They may be very good at their job, or not, but always endeavor to place your best energy upon the quality of your work and inner wellness. Additionally, create the energetic expressions that are intentionally supportive to your boss, supervisor, manager, or owner. With a higher understanding of your potential to positively impact those around you, know that part of your career fulfillment entails THEIR success.

You are not only showing your capacity to be a high quality employee, but you are displaying a level of integrity that expresses your desires for the success of others as well. Be certain that your motivations are pure, or you will simply be seen as manipulative and insincere. This is not a short-term strategy to gain acclaim and material rewards. This is a demonstration of your purpose and focus on service and contribution. These efforts are internally fulfilling and more naturally supportive toward earning the external rewards you desire.

You may offer virtually any kind of service; work indoors or out, be paid an hourly wage or a salary. Regardless of the details, bring your best energy and intentions to work with you. You can choose to incorporate your highest consciousness – including all of the loving principles detailed in previous chapters.

You may honor your truth, support your balanced and healthy overall life, utilize your self-awareness, and choose to express your loving energy with others. Always lead with your highest integrity and be primarily motivated by the goal of contribution. These are all choices that only you can make.

This is certainly not to say that you won't encounter many external challenges or even internal challenges when you disconnect from your truth. Again, your practice in enlightenment is about awakening from delusion and shifting to mindfulness and accountability, as often as is required. Therefore, what is it that you can do to be better prepared to start your workday from a more loving energetic space?

Do you need to make some empowering decisions in your personal life? This may include the removal of certain unhealthy influences, whether person or habit. Always be accountable for monitoring and correcting any outside energy that is harmful to you.

Do you need to begin your day with healthy practices that encourage your connection to your Authentic Self? Start off by elevating your perceptions of your day (and life). Be connected to your truth, and be inspired by that which is uplifting to you. You can meditate, read a few enlightened passages, and do affirmations or prayer. Tailor your "spiritual" practice to your needs and preferences.

This is inner preparation for outer service. You are reminding yourself that you are more powerful than the human problems you perceive. And even if you are having particularly challenging circumstances at the time, at least you are better prepared for dealing with them from your best energy. Otherwise, you start your day feeling defeated before you even begin.

This is all within your control as a more conscious employee. It is your responsibility to create the conditions of inner wellness as best you can. Sometimes you can make the positive changes that elevate your present situation. And at other times, you must simply work with what is, and focus on shifting your perceptions of a current experience toward a more positive and supportive light.

Maybe you have done all of the inner work that you can conceive of doing, and now consistently go to your job feeling happy and healthy. At yet, once there, you routinely lose your loving energy and feel disappointed, discouraged, or even angry. What can you do?

First and foremost, you must accept the reality of your situation "as it is." You cannot wish away or escape from your experiences. You always are accountable for your energy (thoughts, feelings, words, and actions) in whatever environment you find yourself.

If you feel negatively about yourself, your job, or co-workers, you must learn to recognize the higher truth and lesson for you. In some way you are being shown the need to shift, heal, and grow within. You need to assess your energy with wisdom and determine what must change or evolve. Then, through self-love, trust, and courage, you will take the necessary steps.

Simply blaming or finding fault with others will not support you in creating the circumstances that are more joyful and rewarding. In fact, it is never about "the other person or situation," it is about you. This is where most of us will fall under the control of ego and display our "unconsciousness" at work. Or otherwise, give up or retreat into insecurity and disempowerment, accepting less than that which is supportive and fulfilling.

If you presently notice yourself in this position, learn to be grateful instead of fearful (a great way to shock your ego). After all, awareness is the first step to transformation. Learn to discern exactly what is causing this inner fear and pain. If it is essentially "everything" about your job (or life), then you have some significant changes to make.

Sometimes we have to be completely honest with ourselves and admit that we are in the wrong place. It is likely that your intuition has been telling you this for some time, yet it is your outer experiences that are now revealing that which you previously failed to act upon. With awareness, you may now notice a sufficient level of negativity and suffering that you can no longer ignore. As with a destructive relationship, the answer for you may be to move on. But do this in the most conscious way – from the space of self-love and integrity.

If you determine that there are certain specific conditions of your job that are disturbing your energy and minimizing your success, then instead of leaving the job, seek to understand your involvement with these problems. As an employee there are things we can control and many other things we cannot. As you endeavor to be more responsible for your own wellness at work, you must determine your best approach.

There are essentially three things you must do on the enlightened path of consciousness: 1) Change your perception; 2) Change an external condition; 3) Accept what you cannot change and release your negativity around this issue. Virtually all challenging work situations will require varying degrees of these three things. And in all cases the key principle is to choose love over fear.

I like the following phrase: "When you have a choice to be right or be kind (and you always have a choice), choose to be kind." Clearly this addresses the elevation of Spirit and the decline of ego. The need to be "right" requires others to be wrong, in order for us to feel powerful.

Within your higher identity, you will choose what is right and true for you, and then abide in your own love and power. And you may allow others to live within their truth. By the way, choose kindness for yourself (as well as others). At times you are likely your worst critic, and this is unsupportive to your wellness and ascension.

When you are working within the flow of inner-strength and wellness, you will determine what is best for you. Claim your empowerment by honoring your truth, and by taking responsibility for you, without the need to convince or combat others. This is the enlightened path for improving your work situations.

Again, you are assessing a circumstance that is temporarily troubling to you. And you now do this through the perspective of love not ego. If you find that there is no "real" problem, and instead merely a false perception of one, then you must endeavor to shift and elevate your view.

This is the solution more often than you may have realized. In our unawakened state, we have tended to bring our baggage to work (and then we bump up against someone else's baggage). We are clouded by some past memory, self-defeating belief, or false teaching about others. And then when some innocuous event takes place that triggers our delusion, we may express our energy in negative ways.

We actually created a problem within our own mind that did not really exist. With greater awareness you will notice when you or others have done this. However, while unaccountable for yourself, you will just blame them for your problems.

What if you determine that there is a real challenge that seems to require some action to resolve? Then ask yourself, "Is this something within my control to resolve in a mutually supportive way?" Or otherwise, "Is it wholly outside of my control to positively impact?"

If you determine that it is within your ability to transcend some challenge at work, consider your options carefully, through the lens of consciousness. This may have involved some unsatisfactory interactions with certain co-workers, or some detail or condition that adversely impacts the quality of your work. Always take a full view of the situation, integrity is the key. You co-exist with other employees; therefore, you want to promote mutual support whenever possible. Consider the impact of your words and actions upon the others involved.

Next, bring solutions, not problems or accusations. If you do not have a solution, at least bring an energy that is open to one. The worst thing is to be closed off and negative, expecting someone else to solve your problem. That will get you nowhere, and will only discredit your reputation with co-workers. Use your best communication skills. Speak your truth, but be willing to listen to what others are saying. There is likely common ground and consensus available.

If instead, you determine that your grievance is outside of your control to change, then you go within to find peace and acceptance for "what is." Often the most caustic place at work is within our own mind when we desperately want something to be different than it is. Within all of the inter-workings of your company there are a great many things outside of your control. **Honor this truth!** This will foster acceptance and peace, rather than judgement and suffering.

This may reflect your greatest challenge in personal accountability. It often seems easier and more natural for us to focus on the "doing," and much harder to allow for the "being." Ego wants to control, not only us, but others as well. Spirit knows that your inner state of wellness (self-love, self-worth, awareness, integrity, compassion, etc.) is what is most important to your success. Ego wants to be "right" (by its warped definition) while Spirit guides you to be loving, kind, and happy.

When changes or events impact your employer that is outside of your control you must be able to accept them. You may feel happy, angry, disappointed, or whatever, and it is okay to feel what you feel – temporarily. Yet, for the sake of your wellness you must release any negative energy that disturbs your peace and/or your focus on contributing your best.

Or, if you determine that the conditions exist that make it impossible for you to succeed, you must pursue other options. You cannot control all external situations, but you can learn to be mindful, and shift to the perceptions and actions that are healthy and supportive. This leads to consciously choosing love over fear. This acceptance of "what is" leads directly to a more enlightened view of the situation.

Being a conscious employee is about approaching your work from the place of your greatest inner wellness. Delight in doing your job the best you can in order to contribute your highest quality and integrity. Honor yourself by expressing loving energy within the daily functions of your job, interactions with stakeholders, or other conditions surrounding your employment. And create the best balance within your personal life, while supporting career fulfillment.

Conscious Managers and Owners

As manager you are still an employee, but your responsibilities extend beyond that of non-management personnel. Within most companies, owners are a part of management, and in this case, they are ultimately responsible for all that takes place in and for their company. Therefore, because you are higher on the organizational chart, your level of contribution and service must be significantly higher than other employees. And, by virtue of your position of influence over others, you are even more responsible for your expressions of energy.

This accountability will be honored in a conscious business culture. Yet, it is more common that the highest positions enjoy significantly higher compensation, while the integrity and contribution part is "hit and miss." The truth is that historically it has taken truly exceptional people to ascend to a level of higher integrity AND business achievement. An all too familiar path in rising to the top has been primarily based upon one's ability to self-promote and manipulate the system.

The good news is that this is beginning to change. It's time to make consciousness, within business models and practices, the accepted norm. The roles of a diverse and expanding cross-section of society, as well as, the value we will now afford them, are part of our evolution. And this is shifting the business culture. In its highest definition, business is established to serve the needs of society – individually and collectively. And when this is not happening, change is required. Of course, this is very challenging to those who have historically wielded all of the power.

Therefore, as the rights of all individuals are honored, the power will shift to those who live within the principles of Unity Consciousness. Those in leadership positions will bring a broader perspective of possibility, creativity, skill sets, and benefit to all. This is the focus on loving service and contribution that will spell greater success and fulfillment.

As a manager or owner in this new age, your level of consciousness and inner wellness will be more supportive than ever before. Part of this transition will come from a demographic change in leadership (gender, age, race, etc.), and part from the awakening of more individuals. Unfortunately, another aspect motivating this evolution will be less peaceful, coming from so many who have been marginalized and oppressed in our society.

The key for such a shift is in the rising up of enlightened entrepreneurs and managers. The higher you are in the organizational chart the greater your sphere of influence within the company, and thus, the greater your responsibility toward your subordinates. Just as they said in the movie *Spider Man*, "With great power comes great responsibility." Therefore, instead of looking to get rich or make a quick and easy buck, on the backs of hardworking people or their misfortune, integrity is the key.

This level of higher integrity must be reflected in your actions and examples, and not simply a part of your rhetoric. By the way, this must be the standard for all leaders, including our politicians. People always know (eventually) when you are conning them with your words. Quite literally, executive managers and owners must begin to transcend their egos for the betterment of all, including themselves.

Remember, this more conscious approach is the representation of your true identity, power, and light. Therefore, you are not only supporting the wellness in others, but you are making the greatest investment in your own higher fulfillment and ascension. Conscious business leaders will effectively combine their ambition and meaning, within their work contributions.

As an owner, you are betting on yourself and willing to take risks to develop or operate a company. This entitles you to the potential for considerable compensation based upon the success of the whole company. However, it should not come from any mistreatment, misappropriation, or diminishment of value toward any stakeholders.

Conscious individuals with leadership potential will utilize their great energetic ambition in the pursuit of endeavors that support a higher meaning and purpose. You may bring solutions, through business activities, which resolve great human challenges. This is the larger view of finding meaning within the fulfillment of your ambition.

Company executives must be willing to define their success to include the greater support and elevation of others. This includes sharing the financial prosperity and opportunity. This has the great benefit of encouraging participation, contribution, and hope for so many people. All of this is good for business, and business leaders.

Here is the question: Are your ambitions based in Spirit-Love or Ego-Fear? The world needs conscious leaders. If leadership is a part of your unique gifts, skills, interests, and purpose, then endeavor to lead with integrity and love toward all. While this requires your greatest inner strength and wellness, it ultimately provides you with fulfillment on a level that is unmatched by the old selfish standards.

When your primary goals are for income, status, and power, you will typically lose sight of the higher energetic considerations and benefits. Consequently, you may enjoy a comfortable lifestyle without, but experience anxiety and a lack of value within. In your relatively unconscious state this may not immediately disturb you. However, your life will progress along a path that brings the consequences from this lower energetic form, and you will experience conditions that bring a level of suffering.

I am saying that the greatest obligation for elevating consciousness falls upon those with the greatest influence. Living and functioning within the old "status quo" is our path to continue this system that unreasonably enriches the wealthiest few while disabling the many. This is not only unconscionable but unsustainable. Ultimately, desperate people will be required to take desperate actions for the sake of survival.

I have heard discussion in my career about turning over the organization chart. In other words, the higher positions are on the bottom instead of the top, which places them subordinate to all of the "lower" positions. Of course, no one has ever suggested that this translate into the compensation model.

This is an interesting idea, but it takes so much more than lip service and a new visual. It begins with a true awakening of consciousness from the ownership down, and must be a practical reflection of your expressions of loving energy (thoughts, words, feelings, and actions). Ultimately, executives must set aside (or defer) their focus on self-enrichment.

Everything that you do or say, at some point, is seen or known by those who work below you. If you are not operating with full integrity they will know. Some employees will even be waiting for you to fail; endeavor to prove them wrong.

You may think that you are fooling people, but your inner energy manifests in ways that tell the truth. Your words must be impeccable, and your actions must align with your words. Your inner wellness and level of consciousness will translate into the way you treat all stakeholders.

Therefore, endeavor to earn and show respect to those who work under you. Literally, a part of your job is to get the best work out of these employees. Take this responsibility seriously and sincerely. Not just for what you can gain materially, but for all of the ways that you can positively influence someone else's life. You are fulfilling your unique gifts, and this includes leader, teacher, mentor, motivator, and more.

The big question is: Why do you want to be a manager or owner? Are your motivations appropriately balanced between contribution and reward?

You see, I am trying to establish that you have a much greater responsibility than the typical employee. I would not expect anyone to necessarily give back part of their salary; yet, I would like to eliminate a sense of entitlement to wealth simply because of position. I have seen and heard of too many cases where the focus is clearly upon accumulating wealth at the expense of others, and their actual focus on contribution is minimal or measured.

There are different types of organizations, and it is up to you to figure out how to apply this wisdom within your specific situation. And as I said previously, your job requires many human relations skills, beyond the specific work related knowledge. This is not always easy, and it is not for everyone. You will oversee a number of unique human beings, functioning within various levels of consciousness, skill, and integrity. And likely, you have your own boss, to whom you will report.

Once again, the most conscious organizations will be run by conscious leaders at the top. However, this may or may not be the case for you. And, if you are not in a position to change the overall culture, you can at least do your part to elevate your situation. You will have to develop your own higher alignment and consciousness within the way that you honor yourself and others.

As always, you start with your own inner healing and wellness. You must endeavor, through wisdom, mindfulness, and accountability to elevate your self-love and inner-strength. Regardless of any external circumstances, it is your responsibility to develop and bring your best energy to work every day. Accordingly, all of the principles detailed in the previous chapters apply.

However, as a leader, you will require even greater consciousness in order to function on this higher level for the betterment of all. You can see why the easier route is to ignore your own need for inner healing and growth, and simply "boss" others around as a way of meeting your job requirements. I hope that you have witnessed enough of this example in the world to realize that easy is not better, and that as a leader you are following a higher calling.

Work with your subordinates (a work hierarchy term, not a human distinction) as if you care as much about their success as you do your own. In truth, your success and progress is largely dependent upon these co-workers. And they will be more willing to focus on their contributions when they are not fighting for respect, approval, and dignity. This is an example of how embodying the quality of love at work is more supportive to your sustained success than just looking out for your own selfish interest.

A large part of your contribution will come from developing and supporting your staff. And when you lead this endeavor with integrity, you will express a consistently positive message to others. Of course, in addition to this part of your job you will have other duties and external pressures.

Within my experience in management, I worked primarily for companies in their early developmental stages, where we grew from small to medium size. My biggest challenge was that in addition to being responsible for staff, I had my own accounting and corporate responsibilities. Plus, I was involved in developing systems and procedures to accommodate our growth. Consequently, at times, my direct involvement in managing staff was relatively minimal.

I always felt that this was unfortunate, and that so much more could have been done with a greater bandwidth for managing others. Beyond the desire to be a good manager, this is sometimes a factor of budget constraints, skill sets, or organizational philosophy. Yet, any true sense of success will come from adequate management – including oversight, review, policies and procedures, hiring and training practices, emotional support, etc.

Know that there are no perfect or easy scenarios. You will likely be required to balance your time and effort as employee and manager the best you can under the circumstances that exist. However, this also highlights the need for the ownership to prioritize and accommodate the needs of their company over their own short-term gain. Each situation is different, yet, there are often solutions to operational inefficiencies, leading to healthier growth and success, when the owners are willing to take a more conscious approach.

As a manager you want to give your staff the tools and support they need to flourish, and this is always in the best interest of the company overall. However, the owners must give the managers the tools they need to best facilitate their role and competency, which again, is in the best interest of ownership. Everyone is inter-dependent in business, which is why an approach based in love and Unity is the only real solution.

Career Fulfillment

The owner(s) should have the most difficult and responsible job of all. Essentially, their job is to facilitate and support individual and collective success for all of the employees. They must develop a culture, which comes from their highest integrity that brings people together in pursuit of their best contribution and fulfillment.

When they act in a selfish and entitled manner then this lower energy will permeate throughout their company. And if they are a loving and competent example of leadership, then this is what they will foster in their organization. This level of integrity comes from a position of great inner strength and wellness, and should never be confused with weakness.

In addition to your work with employees, owners represent the company to all outside stakeholders as well. This includes the quality and impact of their goods or services in the marketplace or community, relationships with customers, vendors, lending institutions and other business professionals. Accordingly, success in this position requires a great exertion of both a higher quality AND quantity of energy.

Managers and owners must be leaders. You must first learn to lead yourself; therefore, self-mastery is crucial. For whatever your need for inner healing and wellness, your fear and ego-control will manifest as situations fraught with challenge and suffering. So connect to your Authentic Self and work on your inner transformation. This is how you begin to elevate your consciousness, which then may be integrated into all aspects of your life.

So, you still think that you want to own or run a company. Be certain that this is in alignment with your true inner gifts, interests, passion, and purpose. This is not the place for a shortcut to power and prosperity. In fact, if this is your true motivation you will be sorely disappointed. Yet, if this is your calling and path of wellness and fulfillment, you will find a tremendous opportunity to make a difference.

Consciousness for the Self-Employed

We all start out as employees as we begin our career. Some will move up the ranks and find their fulfillment in management or ownership. A path of ownership that is more accessible to many people is to work as self-employed. Typically this implies a one-person company, where you are responsible for all of the business tasks and decisions.

As with any career classification, it is highly supportive to your fulfillment and success to develop and function from the space of higher consciousness. We typical choose this form of career when we have identified and developed a marketable skillset that lends itself to the generation of our personal income. And while this affords us the control and autonomy we may desire, it should also involve participation in a service or cause that has a deeper meaning to us.

Hopefully we have prepared ourselves for the multitude of challenges involved and competencies required. It is in this light that your inner wellness and spiritual integration is quite relevant. Your integrity and self-awareness will be critical to your success and satisfaction.

What is your motivation for owning and running your own business? Is the specific skill that you are selling in alignment with your unique gifts, interest, qualities, and passion? Do you have access to sufficient funding to get you started and keep you going? Do you have the business acumen and contacts to support you where needed?

This is not a good option just because you are tired of having a boss. And don't make the mistake of thinking that this is easier than being an employee because theoretically you can make your own schedule. For nearly everyone who attempts this path, your better option for attaining more security and income is to work for someone else's company.

So, your purpose for selecting this option must be in alignment with your higher truth. You must be inner-driven, self-motivated, and very passionate about your business. It must be treated as a higher calling, one that satisfies your deepest desires for service and fulfillment.

Your higher consciousness will support you in staying the course when things get tough. You will use integrity as the very characterization of your business, and by association, your personal reputation. Your inner-strength will support you while facing the vulnerability of being responsible for business functions outside of your skillset or comfort zone.

Your focus will be upon service and contribution, or you won't be in business long. In this sense, these qualities are not optional (compared to working for someone else). And with all of the ongoing demands, you will need to create the space for holistic wellness (physical, mental, emotional, and spiritual) and life balance.

If you are drawn to start your own business as a way of doing something you love, and you are enthusiastic about growth and ascension, then you may find great fulfillment within this platform. Your first "business" step is to create a realistic and supportive business plan. The details and "how-to" of doing such a plan are readily available from books or the internet.

Beyond the considerations of your initial setup and operational needs, it is best to plan for steady, long-term growth and success. Yet, it will be your focus upon offering your best energy in the present that will have the greatest impact on your fulfillment. Within the establishment of my self-employment, as Author-Teacher-Mentor, this is the strategy I have engaged.

I have envisioned a direction and path of growth for my business. Yet, if I was to spend too much time planning, forecasting, goal-setting, worrying about future results, etc., I would not be as productive or efficient today. My power lies within a connection to my Authentic Self in the present moment. This allows me to focus on the job at hand, which is a mental and spiritual discipline that maximizes my potential. I find success to be a combination of the willingness to trust and honor purpose and productivity in the present moment, along with the ongoing expansion and growth of my skillset.

You must plan and work within your greatest strengths, aptitudes, and purpose. Yet, it is always true that your power is in the present moment. Plans are guidelines based upon your best information and understanding at the time. However, as energy moves, conditions within and without us change. Have a solid plan, but honor the present, and if appropriate, be prepared to be flexible and adapt.

Some services easily lend themselves to self-employment. There are many examples, real estate agent, personal trainer, massage therapist, writer, artist, consultant, and many more. Often you will be able to work within a low-overhead environment. Yet, in addition to offering your specific skill, you will have marketing, accounting and taxes, insurance, IT, banking, legal, and other outside services. Even while not necessarily doing this work directly, you will be responsible for it all.

Enjoy the process, because it is ALL process. The results will follow of their own accord, as a consequence of your energy.

Apply your highest consciousness in order to create your greatest joy, satisfaction, and success. Endeavor to take care of yourself and your clients. Create a framework of peace in your mind, and simply do your best. In truth all things are temporary, even if they feel like "life or death" at the time. Everything is an experiment and lesson in growth and ascension.

Plan to be patient while still offering your best contribution – this is the long-term view of your business opportunity. Often, things will take time to develop. In your startup plan, prepare to cover all of your basic needs, and then also, a substantial contingency fund. Financial considerations may be your greatest outside impediment.

If need be, you can begin to plan and save for your company while retaining your full-time job. Or, as you get started, you may decide to work as an employee part-time, just to help support you while you are developing yourself and your business. There is no one-way to do things. Find your way, in alignment with your truth and higher principles.

There are no guarantees, so simply do your best. Endeavor to enjoy the process each day. Be patient and positive, finding appreciation in this opportunity to live out your dream. The joy and reward may be tremendous, even while the commitment is extensive. Applying your consciousness in the operation of your own business will afford the potential for career fulfillment and meaningful contribution into the world.

CHAPTER 29
Supporting Unity in Business

"There are two ways of spreading light: to be the candle or the mirror that reflects it."

- Edith Wharton

Unity is a key concept within any consideration of enlightenment. Therefore, it has a prominent place in all of my books in this series. Relating to Career Fulfillment, it is a more selfless approach that supports you in connecting with other people from a perspective of greater appreciation of their value and yours. This is a significant factor in establishing that your higher purpose is Service – leading to Success.

Until we can value and honor ourselves, we won't be willing or able to accept the higher worth of all others. Within this lower perspective, humanity degenerates into great fear, judgment, division, discrimination, and suffering. As this takes place within the workforce it impacts opportunities, economics, personal fulfillment, and the greater value and meaning of our life.

By definition, Unity is: Oneness; A condition of harmony; and the quality or state of being made one. As a concept, Unity represents the collective, whether we are talking about humanity as a whole, our entire company of employees, or are immediate group of co-workers. What is truly good for one is beneficial to all; things like tolerance, consideration, and support. What is bad for one is harmful to all;

conditions like discrimination, selfishness, and disempowerment.

As mentioned in the previous chapter, the greatest supporters or detractors of Unity hold titles at the top of the organizational chart. By their expressions of energy (thoughts, words, feelings, and actions) they will set the tone for all others. Therefore, conscious businesses do not exist without conscious ownership and management.

Unity is always encouraged and supported within the conscious business model. It would be the goal of all involved to desire for each team member to rise to their best level of contribution, fulfillment, reward, and success. We know that within this environment the whole company benefits. More opportunities are created for growth and ascension, both personally and professionally. Within this model each person is more supported and accountable.

We may not individually rise at the same time or rate. Yet, we are encouraged by those who are succeeding, and know that in some way we have contributed. And for our part, as we ascend at work, we are proud of our accomplishments without being boastful or egocentric. We are humble, and appreciate the whole team. Our value comes from contributing our best, and not from the distinction of our rewards, income, or title.

In this environment, if anyone does not want to be responsible for contributing their best, this will be obvious and unacceptable to their co-workers and management. They will stand out in a negative way, and be required to recognize that their dissatisfaction comes from their work or attitude, not other people holding them back. From there, you may offer counsel and determine if they can be guided and supported to do better. This is a way to both help the individual who may be struggling, and elevate the quality of the overall organization.

Enlightenment seeks to expose the darkness. You do this through awareness, caring, kindness, and attention. This is not the job of a select few "conscious" employees. It is for the whole company, especially its leaders, to rise to this higher standard.

Unity is an approach that functions within the energy of love, and it values each individual while creating a cohesive group. Moreover, within its ability to do so, it supports and encourages each individual to recognize their own value. Accordingly, the employee's best focus will now be upon service, contribution, and fulfillment.

The opposite business approach is to only really value the executives, and then consider the others to be easily replaceable. In other words, their employees are treated as pawns in their race for personal gain. In this environment, we pay the top employees an amount that leaves very little left in the budget to support the rest, or effectively operate the company.

Consequently, many employees feel abandoned, overworked, and under-appreciated. And, something that has always been short-sighted to me is that these "lower level" employees often have a significant amount of contact with customers and other stakeholders. This is just not good business, by any standard.

Therefore, we must be willing to consider and value the needs of all employees. In order to function and contribute their best we must provide adequate training, clearly defined standards, oversight, encouragement, and feedback. And beyond this, a conscious business will utilize greater awareness within the hiring process, due to a stronger culture of integrity.

As an organization, you are either creating the conditions for contribution, growth, and ascension for all employees who are willing to do their best, or you are hindering these things. Doesn't it make sense that supporting Unity in business leads to the greatest employee satisfaction, production, value to customers, and sustained profitability? Or, do we continue to just focus our objectives upon the entitlement and creation of wealth for top management?

From the realms of higher consciousness, this is clearly a no-brainer. Yet, it takes real people, functioning within a more enlightened perspective, to instigate and create the changes needed. We need more conscious employees at all levels, but especially as business leaders and decision makers.

In Unity or Oneness, your perspective is to do your specific job to the best of your ability as a way of serving, supporting, and enriching yourself and the collective group. Can this always be done perfectly? No. Perfection does not exist, only sincere intention and effort. Yet, on the enlightened path it is your ongoing choice to align with the fulfillment of a higher standard.

As employees, while you cannot necessarily define the culture of the business, you can define your philosophy or expression of energy toward all others. In the work that you do each day, consider the impact, both directly and indirectly, upon your co-workers and the organization.

Act as if what you do truly matters to the success of the company – because on some level or other it does!

Do your best to honor yourself and focus on your contributions, this is an elevation in consciousness. Expressions of Unity and love are the reflection of your inner state of wellness. So, as you endeavor to heal, honor, and love yourself, you will develop this greater capacity that serves others.

A positive perspective of your job and consideration of your co-workers has a very real and positive impact on the energy all around you. You will elevate your surroundings.

Your negativity will have the opposite impact, one that is destructive to the well-being of you and those around you.

These are things that you likely know intellectually. Yet, while you are largely disempowered and stuck in ego-control, the quality of your expressions will be "hit-and-miss" at work, depending upon outside influences. With some honest self-reflection, I am sure that you will notice this as your truth.

Through self-mastery, the higher quality of your energy is more inner-generated, and less susceptible to your outer conditions and interactions. Through awareness, mindfulness, and practice you can transcend your habitual and false mental programming. Enlightenment guides you to learn, define, and create your own path of wellness, satisfaction, and fulfillment. Therefore, within all of your career pursuits, seek your *Enlightened Path.*

PART III: Exercises

1) Take a minute to focus on your current career. Can you determine if you are primarily functioning within one of the three stages (Discovery, Developmental, or Realization)? Accordingly, utilize the most appropriate wisdom from Chapters 19 – 21, in order to gain greater insight and guidance leading to more joy, empowerment, and fulfillment.

2) Within your most truthful inner assessment, determine your greatest motivation connected to your work. Are you primarily aligned with loving principles, like service, contribution, and integrity? Or are you overly attached to ego, and focusing on material gain, recognition, and/or least effort? Notice how this motivation impacts your enjoyment and fulfillment at work. If needed, begin to shift and realign your inner perspective and choose to honor your true self.

3) Analyze the challenges you are currently facing regarding your work/career. Can you see where a greater employment of self-awareness and consciousness would guide you to a healthy resolution? Also, how are you currently supporting your greatest career growth and ascension? Whether through elevated attitude or action, can you find ways to further support your fulfillment and the principles of Unity at work?

PART III: **Affirmations**

I AM now creating and supporting my unique career path.

I AM perfectly designed to contribute my best gifts to the world.

I AM discovering (developing or realizing) my career path through the higher wisdom within.

I AM now expressing the energy of integrity in all that I do.

I AM fully supported at work as I offer my support to all others.

I AM contributing my best energy at work as part of my growth and ascension.

I AM realizing my greatest rewards through higher contribution.

I AM continually guided at work by my higher self-awareness.

I AM elevating my consciousness within my role as employee.

I AM elevating my consciousness within my role as manager/owner.

I AM connecting with my Authentic Self as I promote and support Unity.

ABOUT THE AUTHOR

Scott E. Clark brings his own practical life experience and inner guidance into his writing. He has learned valuable life lessons leading to his own ongoing transformational development. Some of his roles, titles, relationships, and responsibilities, include son, father, grandfather, husband, friend, employee, manager, business owner, student, teacher, mentor, and author.

The highest intention of his writing and teaching is to offer a philosophy and path that may guide others to recognize their true potential through wisdom, mindfulness and personal accountability. This is attained through inner healing and growth, and then expressed out into the world. Even while spending 30 years in the corporate world, primarily in accounting management, his passion introduced him to the higher principles and possibilities of life.

His foundation in spiritual understanding is to include and accept all people as equal spiritual beings who are each on their own unique path of consciousness and evolution. It is from this perspective and energy that he has written, *"On the Enlightened Path,"* as the inspired message he has been guided to share. His natural inclination toward balance, logic, and practicality serves his purpose of introducing the integration of spiritual principles into everyday life.

Current and future books in the *"On the Enlightened Path"* series will address the topics of: Self-Mastery, Relationships, Career, Health, Parenting, and more.

Mr. Clark recognizes that there are many road maps to higher wisdom and inspiration, and for each of us it is a matter of finding our own path of truth. Some examples of the various ancient and contemporary books and wisdom teachings that have inspired him on his journey are:

Buddhism, A Course in Miracles, Kriya Yoga, Tao Te Ching, The Bhagavad Gita, The Yoga Sutras, The Power of Now, The Four Agreements, The Law of Attraction, and many more.

Mr. Clark is also the author of, "The Empower Model for Men: a guide to more conscious living," published in 2014. After his extensive professional business career, as an accountant and financial manager and CPA, he now serves as an author, teacher, and mentor in the field of personal growth and holistic wellness. Aside from the fulfillment of his work, Mr. Clark engages in a daily meditation practice and fitness routine. As he continues to fulfill his higher purpose in service to the world, he cherishes time with his children, grandchildren, family, and friends.